FINALLY, HE PROPOSES...

She accepts.

For a few moments the two lovers share the sublimity of their perfect love. The groom glows with happy contentment and nuzzles his chosen one. The quiet ecstasy of the moment is all that he had dreamed it would be. Then she rises silently from the couch, her smile assuring she will be back in but a moment. She goes to the kitchen, and he thinks of champagne...

She puts on a pot of coffee and sharpens a pencil.

"Let's make a list!"

It's only a hint of the torture to come...

OTHERWISE
Engaged

Alison and Thomas Hill

WARNER BOOKS

A Warner Communications Company

Ⓦ A Warner Communications Company

Printed in the United States of America
First Printing: May 1988
10 9 8 7 6 5 4 3 2 1

Book design by Richard Oriolo
Cover design by Barbara Buck
Cover illustration by Cameron Eagle

Library of Congress Cataloging-in-Publication Data

Hill Alison.
Otherwise engaged.

1. Weddings—United States.   2. Betrothal.   I. Hill,
Thomas.   II. Title.
HQ745.H54   1988   392'.4   87-34528
ISBN 0-446-38702-9 (pbk.) (USA)
ISBN 0-446-38703-7 (pbk.) (Canada)

DEDICATION

*To the Mother-of-the-Bride,
who made it seem almost easy. With love,
respect, and a not inconsiderable
measure of awe.*

Contents

ACKNOWLEDGMENTS

Thanks to our editor Bob Miller, the funny word man; to Cameron Eagle, the funny picture man; and to all unwitting contributors, i.e., our married friends.

Introduction

First comes love, the schoolyard poets sing. Then comes marriage. Oh, if it were only that simple! What they have left out, of course, is engagement.

Falling in love is easy. So is being married. Engagement is the part that causes all the trouble. It's the awkward, in-between stage, like junior high school. Everyone had a lousy time in junior high.

Luckily, here's help. *Otherwise Engaged* is more than just the perfect wedding planner. It offers solace, understanding, even inspiration for the anxious bride- and groom-to-be. For example, there is "Choosing the Right Religion . . . for a Beautiful Ceremony." And don't miss "Your Wedding Dress: What It Says About You." Plus, we promise that diligent use of our nine-week Argument Planner will assure that everything goes off without a hitch.

After our own engagement and wedding we knew we only had two choices: to write this book or to go on *The Newlywed Game.* We decided on the book. This way we can check our answers with each other beforehand, though we really could use the dinette set.

To the groom-to-be: Congratulations. To the bride-to-be: Best wishes. To both of you: May all your days be circus days!

OTHERWISE ENGAGED

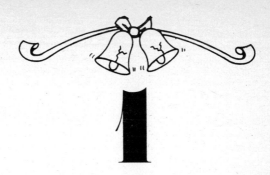

1

The Proposal: Bury My Heart at Bended Knee

THE ENGAGEMENT CRUNCH: WHAT ARE YOUR CHANCES?

The now infamous marriage statistics out of Harvard hit the modern woman like a tidal wave. The conclusion is simple: every year of postponed marriage dramatically increases the odds of never marrying. Playing the field is suddenly turned into a demographic game of Old Maid.

Now, in its wake, our own research indicates more bad news. Even *after engagement* a woman's statistical chances of actually getting married can be affected by a wide variety of factors.

A SINGLE WOMAN'S CHANCES OF EVER GETTING MARRIED

If she is 25 years old 44%

If she is 30 years old 30%

If she is 35 years old 5%

If she is over 65 years old .... <1%

AN ENGAGED COUPLE'S CHANCES OF EVER GETTING MARRIED

If the caterer is snowed in 64%

If the church counselor gives a long, low whistle when he looks over your Myers-Briggs personality test results 55%

If she has the engagement ring appraised the day after she gets it 50%

Approximately forty percent.

Approximately three percent.

If his old college roommates announce their plan
to picket the ceremony 42%

If an ex-boyfriend drives his motorcycle up the
aisle mid-ceremony 40%

If the mothers of bride and groom wear clashing
colors 35%

If the rehearsal dinner degenerates into a
brawl 27%

If the only wedding date you can agree on is
more than twenty-six months ahead 11%

If, while meeting his in-laws-to-be for the first
time, he gets roaring drunk and insists on doing
his shadow puppets of two rhinoceroses
mating 3%

If, at any time between the engagement and
wedding, either of you accidentally refers to the
other by an old lover's name ....<1%

HEALTHBEAT

WHAT IS HAPPENING TO ME?

There will come a time—if you're reading this, you're probably in the midst of it—when a boy becomes a man and a girl becomes a woman. We call this time *engagement*. You will suddenly realize that your body and mind are changing and growing. At first, you may just feel *weird*, but don't worry, you will soon grow accustomed to the "new" you.

First of all, engagement is perfectly normal. It happens to almost everyone, generally between the ages of twenty and thirty, but sometimes later. If you're a "late bloomer," you mustn't feel that "something is wrong with me." Your internal clock knows when the time is right. Trust it.

The earliest signs of engagement are the most obvious physical ones: irresistible smiling at the sight of babies, an unusually conservative haircut, an itchy ring finger. You may also find your voice changing while you talk to your loved one, reverting to cutesy baby goo-gooing. Later on you will notice some "embarrassing" new feelings: strong urges to open an IRA, nostalgia for college, and disenchantment with the newest wave of rock music. Perhaps most surprising of all is a woman's dawning sense that she *is* her mother, and the man's dawning sense that his girlfriend is *his* mother. Don't be ashamed! Look around—you'll notice that many of your friends are going through the same changes.

What can a young person going through engagement do? Here are a few positive mental attitude tools for your personality workshop:

1. Do something "wild and different" for a change. Gals: Try that bright nail polish. Guys: Splurge on those new tires, get yourself the best for once. Let yourself *go!*
2. Just keep telling yourself "it's only a marriage." Don't think of marriage as an *end* to the carefree halcyon days of impetuous youth; think of it as the joyful beginning of a new life of fiscal responsibility, quiet nights at home, and valuable housewares.
3. Take a break and let yourself be a kid again now and then. Nothing can better ease the tension of engagement than making faces at drivers out the back seat of a station wagon, or collecting baseball cards. Relive your childhood! Build a plastic model car, wet the bed, make bread balls. Why not leave a hank of bubble gum on the bedside table and chew it for breakfast?
4. Smile. Research by Dr. Janet Friesinger at Optimo University has shown that just putting on a happy face can keep you from feeling low.

GETTING TO YES: ASKING FOR HER HAND

As Uncle Dudley, a man seldom out of his cups, will remind the groom six times at the reception, marriage is a long sentence beginning with a proposition.

The first step in proposing is being absolutely certain that she will accept. What good is all your romantic planning if she says, "Gosh, that's really nice of you to say, but I don't really know you that well"? So how does a man know for sure that his ladylove will accept his troth? It's not hard. He sees it in her smile, in her touch, in the faraway look in her eyes when he speaks of renovated basements and lawn care.

Even if he misses these subtle signs, he knows. She has told him in a hundred little ways. He got down on one knee to get something under the couch; she said yes. He asked her to give him a hand; she said yes. He said he would give her a ring that evening; she said yes.

The message gets through. Marriage. He toys with the idea, he chews it over like a curious two-year-old with a Frisbee. He ponders. He grins, gurgles, spits up a little. Then he decides: it isn't something to eat, but he might just like it.

So he knows she will say yes. And getting married seems like the thing to do. Still, the sheer momentousness of the decision clouds his vision of joy. How can he be sure? He hesitates, stalls, ponders some more. Then, impetuously, he decides. Unfortunately and unromantically, this irrevocable decision usually comes not while he is looking into her limpid pools, but while looking into the mug of a balding discount jeweler. Dizzied by a heady mix of economics and emotions, he nods his head and trades in his life's savings for a diamond that won't even play records. With this purchase, the decision is made. Now he just has to ask her.

On the way home, doubts set in. Not in her, in the diamond. The appraiser was obviously the salesman's cousin. The stone is obviously a zircon, a piece of glass, a chunk of worthless pyrite. He tries to remember how it happened. He had just paused to look in the window when

The salesman reeled him in like a 2-pound trout on 200-pound test.

the salesman reeled him in like a two-pound trout on 200-pound test.

In any case, the groom-to-be must now craft a plan. Nobody ever just "popped" the question. Proposing is not an impulsive business. What are the perfect moment, the perfect words, the perfect means to ask for the lady's hand? Should he be whispering in a moonlit café over a bottle of Château Lafite? Perhaps a breathless proposal while running down an up escalator? Is skywriting appropriate? Here are some basic tips:

DO write a love sonnet with adorably bad rhymes.

DON'T send your proposal via Balloon-a-Gram.

DO pick a romantic environment: ice skating, a boat ride, a hike through the countryside.

DON'T leave your proposal on the answering machine if she's not home.

DO rehearse your lines carefully.

DON'T use baseball metaphors to explain how much you love her.

DO have a backup plan if she laughs at you.
DON'T insist.

5 MYTHS ABOUT GETTING MARRIED: ARE THEY TRUE?

You've heard your married friends talk, you've seen shows on television, you've even read articles written by real doctors. Still, you're finding it difficult to sort through all the information: what's fact and what's fiction? Here's the truth about five of the most common myths about marriage.

1. **Marriage is contagious**. True. The trends that are often traced among friends and colleagues cannot be attributed merely to peer pressure or the power of suggestion. Doctors now believe that the marriage bug is for real! The subtle paths of the WED-Complex 2 virus are only now becoming clear to medical researchers, and it will probably be years before a successful vaccine is developed. But don't worry, it's not fatal—unless you're allergic to monogamy!

2. **Married people eat better than single people**. False. Sure, they eat sitting down more often, but that doesn't dictate the food groups you choose. And, of course, once the bride steps into motherhood, the baby makes sure that no one gets a balanced diet around the house. "Grazing," the preferred at-home method of consumption for singles, is, in fact, very nutritious. As single people stand before their open refrigerators, their hands will reach for the foods that their bodies need most. Of course, when you eat at a table, your only choices are what is on the plate in front of you. As for consumption outside the home, singles eat in a greater variety of places, depending on their dates, thus balancing their diets more than married folks do. Plus, because singles often wish to impress their companions, they may order more widely and sensibly, whereas a married person is more likely to say, "I don't care what you say. We *never* have it at home, so I'm having three orders of cherries jubilee for dinner!"

3. **Married people are physically unable to dance.** False. This belief, once supported by doctors, has been used by many a new husband. Modern medicine has now proved decisively that marriage does not in any way affect one's ability to dance.

4. **Married people's faces never break out.** True. A hormone released by the pituitary as you repeat your marriage vows will course through your body until the day you die. This hormone, a true miracle of nature, keeps your skin as clear as in your prepubescent years, although it cannot provide the moisture and resiliency of that younger skin. Other results of the so-called "hymeneal hormone" are a tendency to wake up arguing, severe allergic reactions to in-laws, and, of course, the onset of "baby fever."

5. **Married people never have fun vacations.** True. This last is ironic, as married people spend huge amounts of time planning "a really, really fun one, this time." Single people often vacation at the drop of a hat and have a blast, even if it's raining. Married people invariably spend their vacations wondering if they should have gone.

RING-A-DING-DING: HOW TO CHOOSE A DIAMOND

Corporate lawyer or farm gal, waitress or TV repairperson, Jewish princess or Zen Buddhist—every woman wants a best friend, preferably of a carat and a half or more, nothing gaudy, mind you, and just a simple, classic setting. After all, a diamond is roses and ballroom dancing and swing sets and secluded beaches and champagne and homemade cookies all distilled into one tiny dewdrop of pure romance.

If your belle insists that an engagement ring isn't necessary, it's really just her way of saying that if she waited for you to scrape together that much dough, she'd have to use her pension to pay for the honeymoon. Read between the lines, loverboy! What she really means is, "Marry me now, I'll squeeze a ring out of you later."

So just what is this rock going to run you? The Diamond Industry Council provides some simple guidelines, suggesting that you spend 75 percent of one year's salary, or four years' rent, whichever is greater. Perhaps the most sensible system is simply to figure out the most you can possibly afford, and triple it. What's a man to do? There are no easy answers. Insider trading has been heavily touted in the media, but there are plenty of other ways to afford a decent diamond. One charter flight from Bolivia to the

LE MOOD RING
Your barometer of *love*!
Imported. $12.95

THE GAMBLER
She'll be in seventh heaven
Best Buy. $5.95

RADAR HOMING DEVICE RING
Forsake all others—you bet! $15.95
(Batteries not included.)

By Special Order
THE PERMANENT TATTOO RING
I do I do I do! $24.95

The Ever-Popular **SQUIRTING DIAMOND**
Just $4.95!
Our Biggest Seller

HANDCUFF RINGS
Be mine! $5.95

LUCK BE A LADY
The Fabulous "Roulette" Ring
Now $6.95

CHINESE HANDCUFFS RINGS
His 'n' hers. The more you pull,
the tighter they get. A million laffs. $5.95

LUCKY U
Whatta Deal! $2.95

Florida Keys could take care of all your wedding expenses. However, the more prison-conscious groom-to-be might look to the state lotteries, where a one-dollar investment can be worth millions.

After you've raised the ransom, shopping for the diamond can be a perilous business. For example, many less-than-scrupulous jewelers will tell you to look for the four C's: cut, clarity, color, and carat. This deceptive practice will not bamboozle customers who know the *real* four C's of diamond buying:

1. ■ **Cost.** Look at price tags first, diamonds second.

2. ■ **Capital.** What have you got in the bank? How much longer can you ignore your student loan? How did you do at last week's poker game?

3. ■ **Credit.** Does he offer an installment plan? VISA means you can stretch out your payments for a couple of years. Amex is good for a month or two leeway.

4. ■ **Compensation.** Is your chosen lady going to appreciate your extravagant purchase? Estimate how many dinners, movies, and drinks you can get her to pay for during the initial glow of the engagement, and deduct those from your purchase price to arrive at your actual cost.

LOVE ON THE INSTALLMENT PLAN

You simply cannot afford a diamond. "What do poets like us need with money?" you tell your bride-to-be, and you mean it. You return bottles, and not out of environmental concern. You're trying to cut back on how many newspapers you buy. Still, you want to give her something special on the day you propose. Don't despair! Love will find a way. Here are just a few snazzy ideas that won't break your budget.

- A zircon is a boy's best friend. A real, genuine diamonelle is good, too. Just tell her it's a diamond. A few juicy secrets are just the ingredients to keep the sparkle and mystery in your romance for years to come.

- The Emperor's new ring—what could be cuter and sweeter than playing a little make-believe? Describe your gift in glowing detail. What the heck, throw in a diamond tiara and brooch, too.

- Remember the small rock you saved from the beach where you first kissed? Why not mount it in a ring? A simple Tiffany setting will display any pebble to perfection. How about other love tokens? A baby tooth looks ideal in a Royal Mountebank gold band. And choose a Monte Carlo setting to show off a small piece of chrome taken from your '67 Corvette. Hopelessly romantic.

- How about a bubble gum machine ring? It may turn her finger green, but every trip to the grocery store will be an opportunity to renew your vows.

THE ARGUMENT PLANNER

DEBATE OF THE WEEK: Resolved, that she would *not* have accepted a proposal from the old boyfriend if he had asked.

YOUR PERSONAL CHECKLIST	DELAYED	SETTLED	MOOT
1 Is giving her money to buy a ring an acceptable proposal?	☐	☐	☐
2 Were his parents being sincerely happy or just polite when you told them?	☐	☐	☐
3 Is age six too early to start the children on violin lessons?	☐	☐	☐
4 Which of you is "marrying up"?	☐	☐	☐
5 Is it really necessary for her mother to move in with the two of you for the entire engagement?	☐	☐	☐

SYMBOLIC ACT OF REASSURANCE: Meld your record collections.

2

Affianced: The Seven—Day Itch

LOOKING GOOD!
HOW TO IMPROVE YOUR ENGAGEMENT ANNOUNCEMENT

Your first consideration as an engaged couple should be to send your engagement announcement to the newspapers. Start with your hometown papers and your current local paper. But don't stop there! Any places you've summered or towns with relatives should also be contacted. Did you once spend a weekend in San Francisco? The

Chronicle will want to know. And don't neglect other out-
lets: alumni newsletters, magazines, radio and TV. Don't
worry if you're not a Kennedy or a rock star. You'll have
no trouble whipping up a media blitz. Status is just a state
of mind.

But first, you may ask, why does it matter? Independent
laboratory research shows it makes all the difference in the
world. Edgehill University's Department of Engagements
tracked 237 couples from the time of their engagement
announcements to twenty years later. They discovered that
those couples who had poor or no engagement announcements suffered mightily; most were divorced, bankrupt, and
in bad health. The couples who had prime coverage—that
is, at least two newspapers, both with a photograph in the
number-one spot (top right corner, first page, society sec-
tion) and at least five inches of copy—had incomes top-
ping $100,000, were robustly healthy, knew how to tell
jokes, and had great-looking kids.

How can you assure your place among life's "winners"?
The first step is to improve your *careers*. The key here is
to be as mysterious and vague as possible, as though
national security demanded discretion. And you don't have
to lie. If the groom managed to borrow five bucks from
his cheap Uncle Seymour, he surely qualifies as "involved
in international finance." Is the bride a checkout clerk at
the A&P? Try "regional consultant for a food service con-
glomerate." It's as simple as beefing up a résumé—and
you won't even have to explain yourself in an interview.

The next important credential is *education*. Even if you
didn't finish high school, this presents no problems. Make
a point of visiting a prestigious campus. Then you can

honestly note that you "went" there. If you can't make the trip, buy a postcard of a famous university. It's almost the same thing. Then throw in a few academic awards and honors—simply make up a little presentation sheet and have your spouse-to-be hand it to you; in this manner you have, of course, received them.

Next, you'll need to address the problem of *family*. You may say that your family is good enough for you. Well, you're probably right, but they're not good enough for your announcement! They won't be offended once they understand what a difference it can make. Make the bride's janitor-father into "a well-known figure around City Hall," or the groom's mother, a dental hygienist, into "a surgeon who once operated on King Farouk."

Dealing with family brings in more options. Since many members are older, they are even less likely to be checked. Is your grandmother compulsive about doing the dishes? "A nationally consulted authority on hydrodynamics." Did your father like to put together model cars when he was young? How about "engineer of some of the finest auto-mobiles built in the 1940s"?

Why not recruit historical notables as ancestors? They're not going to complain—they're dead. It's important not to be too obvious. Trying "direct descendant of Abraham Lincoln" or "Howard Hughes's firstborn son" is likely to get you into trouble. Instead, go for "grandnephew of the Pretender to the Portuguese throne" or "descendant of Ed-win M. Stanton, Secretary of War under Lincoln." Both of these sound extremely impressive and are much less likely to be challenged. If you share a last name with some minor historical character, all the better.

The final part of this package is the *photograph*. Sometimes, it is simply a matter of retouching the bride's actual engagement picture. If, however, the airbrush is not enough, don't hesitate to send in a photo of someone else. Again, don't be too obvious. Someone is bound to wonder if you send in Nastassia Kinski or Christie Brinkley. Opt for an especially pretty relative or a local model.

By now, you should feel ready to prepare your announcement. Remember—wedding presents will get broken and lost, the bride's dress will yellow, the memories of the event will fade away, but the effects of your engagement announcement will be felt forever. Don't sell yourself short.

*W*EDDING *B*UCKS

Every little bit counts when you're trying to save for a future together! Here's a tip for earning a few extra dollars.

Start taking bets on whether or not your wedding will come off. That's right, be the bookie for your own wedding! By taking a modest house cut, you can end up with a handsome profit, whether or not you end up with a spouse.

Keep excitement—and money—building throughout the engagement by adjusting the odds each time the two of you have a raging battle or passionate reunion. (Not legal in all states.)

Projected Profit: $500–$2,000.

HOW LONG AN ENGAGEMENT? TIME IT RIGHT

In his landmark *English Social History*, G. M. Trevelyan tells of one young woman in the seventeenth century who, "when she hesitated to marry a poor and ugly widower of fifty, was for nearly three months on end 'beaten once in the week or twice, sometimes twice in one day, and her head broken in two or three places.'" In modern-day America, of course, things are very different. Most engagements last much longer than three months. Yet, engagement is still a harrowing and difficult period in the lives of both the bride- and groom-to-be.

Naturally, the foremost consideration in choosing a date for your wedding is how long an engagement it allows. Luckily, there is a simple guideline that can eliminate any possibility of a social gaffe. Choose a day between twenty-four and twenty-eight weeks after the day you went public with your plans.

This rule is neither arbitrary nor some arcane relic of etiquette, but a sturdy compass to guide you through the

20 weeks: too fast.

40 weeks: too slow.

26 weeks: just right.

shoals and whirlpools of the stormy sea that is engagement.

Fine. Try and organize a wedding in twenty weeks. Just don't come crying to us when the only day your church is free is Tuesday afternoon. There is an incredible amount of planning and purchasing ahead—invitations, bands, rehearsal banquet halls, flowers, the trousseau, housing for out-of-town guests—so don't cut yourself short. How would you feel about walking up the aisle in lily-white shoes that, for lack of time, you couldn't dye to match your ivory dress, among guests who received invitations so late they didn't have time to get what you registered for, and be married by a Buddhist priest—the only minister available that day?

On the other extreme, go ahead and set the date for ten months away. Just don't expect anyone to believe that it will actually come off. Want to know what people will be saying when they first hear about the happy event, and the chosen date? "Gosh, when will he quit stalling?" "I understand we have a year after the wedding to get a present— I'm waiting. Why spend perfectly good money on a divorce in the making?" "May twenty-fourth? What, is she trying to let her old boyfriend down gently?"

What's more, engagement is a tense time, an awkward in-between stage for your relationship. The wedding plans will occupy your every waking hour, and your dreams will be filled with infinite aisles, angry priests, and receptions in quicksand. You will be in contact with your parents nightly. Do you really want it to last a year?

PICK THE
RIGHT DATE–FOR YOU

Paula and Mark always had their hearts set on a June wedding, so the evening when Mark "popped the question" they took a quick flip through their calendars and picked June 4. They would rue the decision.

Deborah and Zeke chose January 21. On January 14, when they realized what they had done, the wedding actually had to be delayed.

It was too late for Samantha and Harry to change the date, but their poor planning made a mockery out of their wedding.

Think before you pick a date! There are dozens of disasters that can be so easily avoided. Begin with thorough research. Pick a few possible dates to start. First, check them with major relatives for conflicts. Check with your chosen religion. Christmas is probably out of the question, for example. Catholics can't get married during Lent, Jews can't get married between Passover and Shabuoth, Mormons have to wait a month between marriages.

Another key research method is to read back issues of the newspaper for your chosen town on that date for the past few years. Is there an annual flood? Football homecoming weekend? Shriners' convention? Bikers' rally? Avoid these, if only to make sure there are hotel rooms available.

Finally, consult numerologists, biorhythm experts, or any family members familiar with voodoo or the mystic arts. Why take any chances?

What happened to Paula and Mark? The wedding was to take place in her hometown, Spivey's Corner, North Carolina, a small rural community. They made arrange-

ments with the Presbyterian church that Paula had at-
tended as a child. It seemed perfect—a little out of the
way, perhaps, but a beautiful piece of the country.

Paula had forgotten about Spivey's Corner's one claim
to fame: the annual National Hollerin' Contest. Next door
to the church.

What forced Deborah and Zeke to postpone their wedding? Their original date coincided with a little thing called
the Super Bowl, that's all.

And Samantha and Harry? An outdoor wedding had been
their dream. Foolishly, however, they failed to consult their
Farmer's Almanac and found themselves with 8 million un-
invited wedding guests: a statewide swarm of seventeen-
year locusts.

Pick *your* date with care!

THE MARRY MONTHS

There are many traditional poems that tell what blessings
the various months confer upon a marriage that occurs in
them. This unusual sixteenth-century Gaelic farmer's poem
reflects the yeoman's meager subsistence, while retaining a
hopeful, romantic poignancy.

IF YE MARRY

If ye marry when the year is new,
Swae hops yield a bitter brew.
If in February twa become one,
Ye corn rigs'll wither i' th' sun.
Take yer Kate whilst March does blow,
Aye slow or ne'er the spuds'll grow.
Say yer vows whilst April rains,
A life of worry, aches and pains.

If ye marry in the month of May,
Calamity; disease; decay.
Trot the aisle in month of June,
Ye'll fall to beggin' mighty soon.
When marriage in July is had,
Luck you'll hae, but only bad.
In August take ye wifey's kiss,
Food and drink ye'll sorely miss.
If ye marry in olde September,
Why ye did, ye won't remember.
If October's harvest see your wedding,
Start in now, starvation dreading.
Choose brisk November in which to wive,
What roots ye plant will ne'er thrive.
If the bride be December's daughter,
Yer dinner gruel'll be thin as water.

HEALTHBEAT

MEN: DON'T LET THE POST-PROPOSAL DEPRESSION GET YOU DOWN!

A recently engaged friend of mine moped that "engagement is the only time in a man's life when everyone congratulates him on losing a battle." What could I say? It's not that he was *wrong*, of course, just that he had a *negative attitude*. It's too easy to come down hard after the adrenaline rush of proposing and the exciting flurry of spreading of the news have passed. How can you stay cheerful, with a wedding in the works? Here are a few ideas to cure your blues:

- Cook yourself up a pot of quick macaroni and cheese and eat the whole thing yourself with a warm Budweiser. See? Bachelor life wasn't so great.

- Get involved in the planning. Get on the line while your bride-to-be talks with her mother. Here are grown women giggling and howling and making lists like a prom committee. Feed on their excitement. If that doesn't work, try teasing them about it.

- Invite fewer bachelors to poker night. Who needs those shiftless ne'er-do-wells? You have plenty of married friends who are just as much fun. Just a little quieter. Less blustery. Nothing wrong with that. And the game will be over in plenty of time to get home for the eleven o'clock news.

- Think about all your New Year's Eves past. Miserable, right? At the very least, you will never go dateless again.

- Make a little "private time" just for yourself. Don't let yourself feel burdened by all the preparations. See how many baseball cards you can flip into a hat. Listen to an old Monty Python record. Get a new address book and fill it in. Burn ants up with a magnifying glass.

SHE'S YOUR BEST FRIEND: WHY ISN'T SHE HAPPY FOR YOU?

She's been your best friend since fourth grade. So last week, when he finally proposed, she was one of the first you told. Since then, something's been bothering you, a little voice in the back of your head. What's wrong? You try to recall

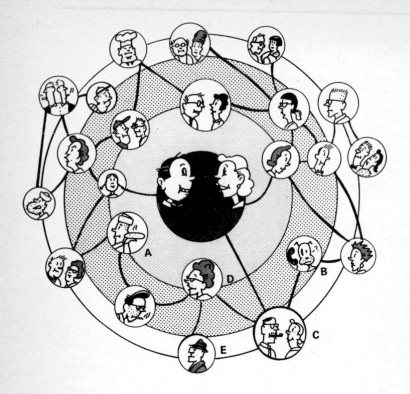

THE "HEARD-YET?" DENSITY FLOW CHART

HOW THE GRAPH WORKS: A PARTIAL GUIDE

Proposal at Ground Zero (A) is interrupted by pizza delivery man, who becomes the first to know. Her parents are not home, but Jocelyn the Dog (B) overhears frantic phone messages on answering machine. His parents are home, playing bridge with the Piltdowns (C) who become the fifth and sixth to know. Aunt Mary (D) calls, quickly discovers engagement, and chalks it up to her psychic intuition. Aunt Mary proceeds to tell her ex-husband Hal (E), her upstairs neighbors, her no-good boyfriend Ted, your Aunt Frieda, a sailorman and everyone else she knows.

KEY

■ Ground Zero
□ Within 15 minutes
▨ 15 minutes to 1 hour

You chose her to share this most special time with, to tell the smallest detail and confidence.

her reaction, and something isn't sitting right. Now that you think of it, she didn't shriek and hop when you told her! In the ensuing hourly phone calls, she seemed to act even odder. You chose her to share this most special time with; to tell the smallest detail and greatest confidence. She's the lucky maid of honor, your partner in planning, a sounding board for your every idea. And yet, she seems strangely distant.

In fact, she isn't acting like your idea of a best friend at all. You could hardly believe it when she objected to you telephoning your Aunt Jenny in Nepal from her house. Why is she trying to put a damper on your joy? Then she asked you to stop dropping by at 4 A.M. to discuss the guest list again. She seems a bit distracted, too, murmuring something about a visit to the hospital just when you were busy describing the adorable little lace cap you'd found in the antique shop. Should you have stopped and asked about *her*? No! *You're* the bride-to-be, *you* are the star. This is *your* time. Yet her behavior continues to be selfish and demanding. What's going on here? Just what kind of a "friend" is she? How could she object to spending $1,200 on a bridesmaid's dress, when you're spending $2,300 on your gown?

As the bride-to-be, *you* are the most important person here. It's imperative that you remember this, and that you gauge your best friend's behavior accordingly: Did she object when your groom called her "fruit-loops"? Did she beg off tying up the four hundred tiny bags of rice all by herself? And lastly, did she object to gaining twenty-five pounds for the wedding day so that you would look slimmer by comparison?

What's the solution? Should you spend precious hours attending to *her* needs and wishes? Certainly not. Dump her.

WEEK EIGHT

THE ARGUMENT PLANNER

DEBATE OF THE WEEK: Resolved, that she likes the *idea* of marriage more than she likes him.

YOUR PERSONAL CHECKLIST

	DELAYED	SETTLED	MOOT
1 Do you still have to pretend you don't live together?	☐	☐	☐
2 What does it mean that his old girlfriend is getting married the same month?	☐	☐	☐
3 Does the engagement require her to supply unlimited celebratory beer to his buddies?	☐	☐	☐
4 Should she take a leave of absence from work to plan the wedding?	☐	☐	☐
5 For $10,000, would you rather have a new car or a nice wedding?	☐	☐	☐

SYMBOLIC ACT OF REASSURANCE: Read an entire issue of *Modern Bride* together.

3

Who's Whose: The Lists

BASEBALL CARDS FOR GUEST LISTS? SOUNDS ZANY, BUT IT WORKS!

The guest list is the most powerful organizing tool available to the modern bride. It serves to check off RSVPs, correlate gifts to guests, cross-reference formal seating, coordinate out-of-towner housing, and also makes a handy set of flash cards for the groom to memorize the bride's distant cousins. The guest list is the key, the hub, the wedding's nuclear core. Without it, you're as good as single.

Patricia Douglas, née Porter
Housewife, traveler, amateur gardener
50s   5'6"   170+

Approx Gift Cost: $40
Bats: Right
Throws: Right

Hattie pinches grown men on the cheek.

Mitch Crandall
Owns local auto dealership
40s   6'0"   190

Approx Gift Cost: $10
Bats: Switch-hitter
Throws: Right

Mitch enjoys golf and fishing.

It's fun to think of Aunt Hattie being Goose Gossage.

You're going to be spending a lot of time with your guest list these next few months. Why not take the time to make it right? At the very least, it has to be on cards. Working on legal pads or wedding planners is hopeless when you start arranging tables or sorting out no-shows. Index cards will do the job, of course, but why stop there?

One snappy idea for a list is baseball cards—it'll get the hubby-to-be involved! Use regular trading cards, but replace the names with those of your possible guests. Change the faces if you like, but it's fun to think of Aunt Hattie being Rich Gossage, just so long as you don't slip and call her "Goose" at the reception. Once you start, you may find yourself adding more details, or "stats." Take EAI (estimated annual income) and divide by ECG (estimated cost of gift) to get each player's GQ (generosity quotient). Don't forget the "fun fact" cartoons: Jerry likes hunting and fishing. Clara lists playing cards and reading among her hobbies.

Once you've got your complete set, you'll have *fun* while you decide who gets to come to the rehearsal and who doesn't!

"I'll give you two college pals for your nephew Brian."

"No way, I've got a complete Keeler family—I'm keeping 'em."

"What if I throw in Donna Wentworth?"

"Hmm . . ."

Don't let honing your guest list become a dull chore, as you dread untwisting the rubber band from the ratty, dog-eared index cards. Make your guest list as individual as the guests themselves!

"EX"-TERMINATION: WHEN SHOULD FORMER LOVES MAKE YOUR LIST?

In the Virginia reel of modern romance, it is not always easy to separate the friends from the lovers. Of course, any "ex" should be X'd off your list. But what constitutes an ex? The best solution—as always—is communication.

So long as bride and groom understand each other, there won't be any sticky situations. To start, take this his 'n' hers compatibility quiz separately, and then compare your answers.

HERS

IS HE AN EX?	**YES**	**NO**

1. You went on one dinner date, to a Pizza Hut.
2. He recorded an album of country songs written about you.
3. You "had a fling" but he has clinical amnesia, and doesn't know it ever happened.
4. In third grade he traded lunch boxes with you.
5. He once accidentally saw down your shirt.

HIS

IS SHE AN EX?	**YES**	**NO**

1. Your parents always wanted you to ask her out.
2. A noted television psychic said you would marry her someday.
3. You've never met her, but did have her centerfold on your wall all through college.
4. She once said she liked your last name.
5. You "had a fling" but then again, it might have been her twin sister.

"Dear Baffled . . ."

MODERN-DAY ENGAGEMENT DILEMMAS WITH DIDI DIVINE

DEAR DIDI DIVINE,　▼

Harry's been impossible about lots of things about planning the wedding, but his latest inspiration takes the cake! He wants his best friend from college—a woman named Clara—to be his *"best man"*! Clara's perfectly nice, but she's also just plain *perfect*—she's 5'10", great figure, long blond hair. What's a bride to do?

—*Baffled in Buffalo*

DEAR BAFFLED,

Oh, my God! Of course, you're right! You'll look like Harry's *pet dog* standing on his other side! On the other hand, you don't want to make a scene with Harry, who's obviously trying to weasel out of your grasp anyway—don't give him an excuse! Drastic measures are called for. Does the ditz live in town? The way to get her out of the ceremony is by temporary disfigurement. Those kinds of girls can't stand to be seen unless they look great. I discovered this because my fourth husband, Sam, wanted to invite his terrific-looking ex-wife (his second) to the wedding. Well, I couldn't argue too much—he'd only agreed to get married after I promised he could use Petey's Rolls (Petey was my second, God rest his soul). Anyway, this absolute *bimbo*—Roxanne, I'll call her—was all excited about coming. It wasn't so much the way she looked that bothered me as how *stupid* she was. I really think she would have brought down the level of the entire celebration. Then a miracle happened! Roxanne got this terrible, terrible sty in her left eye! I swear I didn't have anything to do with it, although Sam claimed that was the beginning of the end of our marriage (it lasted another four months, though). The point is, Roxanne spent my wedding day locked inside that tacky mansion she'd made Sam give her, and *not* at my beautiful wedding!

It's best, of course, not to leave this kind of thing to fate. We girls have to make our own luck! Try something straightforward and effective—poison ivy does a good job. *–Love, Didi*

Dear Didi Divine, ▼

The most awful incident threatens to ruin my wedding day! My grandfather's girlfriend used to go out with my fiancé's great-uncle Ted. You'd think they could handle the situation with maturity (they're all over seventy years old), but Great-uncle Ted claims that he gave Lily (my grandfather's girlfriend) a sapphire ring while they were going out, and now he wants it back. Whenever we repeat this to Lily, she replies, "It was paste, the cheap bastard. I threw it out." Ted swears he'll make a huge scene at the church if Lily doesn't come up with the ring. What's a bride to do? –Desperate in Denver

DEAR DESPERATE,

Talk about coincidences! Almost exactly the same thing happened to me, just a few years ago! Here's what I did. I got Susie, my grandfather's girlfriend, to have a really good copy of the ruby (hers was ruby) ring made. Then she gave it to Luke, my husband's (number six) great-uncle, just before the ceremony! That old drunk couldn't possibly tell the difference—his eyesight was so bad we could have handed him a paper clip with a cherry Lifesaver on it. The ornery coot kept quiet long enough for us to get married (he stayed quiet another two weeks before figuring it out—just as long as Luke and I stayed married). *–Love, Didi*

DEAR DIDI DIVINE, ▼

I'm about to order my husband-to-be's wedding band, and the jeweler asked me if I'd like to have something inscribed inside. It sounds like a sweet idea, but is it too old-fashioned? I never hear of people doing this anymore. *–Hip in Houston*

DEAR HIP,

Old-fashioned! Not at all! In fact, there are some real advantages to getting an inscription. First of all, let me say how glad I am to hear that you are giving him a ring—now, if you could just have it welded to his finger! As for the inscription, it will make it harder for him to hock the ring, of course. Also, any woman that gets close enough to read it (I know that's pretty close, honey, but you might as well face the facts now) will see the date, so for the first year or two, you may ward off sentimentalists—many women don't like to "date" men who are newlyweds.

As for what should be inscribed, the date, as I've mentioned, can be useful. "I place my trust in you" has been known to give a tweak to some men's consciences, while "Don't you dare" tends to egg them on. A simple "Property of _____" will sometimes do the trick. To be utterly practical, you might try "Thanks for the memories" and call it a keepsake ring. *–Love, Didi*

*W*EDDING *B*UCKS

Those twenty-four friends from college that she insists on inviting are adding to the bills! His seventeen boring cousins are all being asked! What's a modern couple to do about all these extra expenses?

Don't *give* the treasured best-man and maid-of-honor slots away—hold an auction and sell them to the highest bidders among your friends! Remember, the rest of the wedding party spots may bring a decent price as well. As for the flower girl and ring-bearer, tots love these roles and may be willing to give up several weeks' allowance for them.

If this idea sounds a bit indelicate, just let word get around that you are finding it difficult to decide who your *closest* friends are. You'll garner free dinners, weekends in the country, and, in some cases, cash bribes.

Projected Profit: $600–$1,000.

Musical Chairs: Winning the Seating Game

Without being crass, it's important to admit that you, or perhaps your family, have invested a considerable amount of money in providing a spectacular meal at the reception —better by far than that poor showing your cousin Amy had. But all those dollars will be for naught if your guests aren't seated right. Ill-chosen groups could easily degenerate into sullen silences, insulting insinuations, shoving and shin-kicking (under the tablecloths), or, worst of all, an out-and-out food fight. So unless you want that pricy poached salmon whizzing by your ear, or those handily sized stuffed cherry tomatoes splattering on the wall, take time now to arrange your guests.

Always use common sense. Don't put your near-alcoholic friend Sharon at a table with your teetotaling Great-aunt Hilda. Ex-spouses who are not friendly with one another should not be put at the same table. Ex-spouses who *are* friendly with one another but have remarried should not be put at the same table. And so on.

Don't seat redheads with blonds. Both must go with brown-haired people. This mistake has been made, unthinkingly, by many. No one knows why, but putting these two together is like mixing ammonia and bleach.

Do not place Jerry Lee Lewis fans at the same table as Joni Mitchell fans. Just imagine!

Never, ever place a Gemini next to a Sagittarius.

When arranging sports fans, do not seat Yankee fans and Red Sox fans at the same table. Yes, it seems obvious, but it's amazing how many people forget, and too many senseless deaths have resulted from this, which puts a real damper on the party.

In order to help you avoid these and other dangers, here is a sample questionnaire to send to your guests along with their invitations. It's imperative that they fill it out completely and return it on time.

1. What is your favorite color?
2. What sports do you like?
3. How much do you drink at social occasions, particularly weddings?
4. Are you a bigot? If yes, please list groups you particularly despise.
5. What do you do for a living?

The Bad Table: the beauty of it is, of course, no one else has to get near it.

6. What colors do you plan to wear to the wedding?
7. Would you rather be a pencil sharpener or a pear? Explain.

In the course of sorting out all your guests into appropriate tables, you will have a few people that you'll put aside repeatedly, each time a little more desperate for a place for them. But you won't find it, because, as you yourself will finally be forced to admit, *you wouldn't wish these people on anyone.* There is, however, the perfect solution: the Bad Table. Your whining roommate from freshman year, the boring new mother with the colicky baby she refused to leave at home, your unceasingly lecherous Uncle Del, the Kleigschmit twins—all of your problem guests placed in one easy step—at one horrible nightmare of a table. The beauty of it is, of course, no one else has to get near it!

QUIZ:
IS YOUR ETIQUETTE ADEQUATE?

Most of us are comfortable with the basics of etiquette, and the basics are really all that are required. Common courtesy, common sense, and all those things your mother taught you will take you a long way. But getting married is a serious matter, so you'll want to be sure the two of you are completely prepared. The quiz below can serve as a checklist, and will fill in any gaps in your knowledge.

INTRODUCTIONS

1. The only one of the following a woman would *not* be presented to is:
   a. A recognized head of state.
   b. An elderly, well-respected man in the community.
   c. The youngest daughter of the King of Spain.

2. A guest in a box at the opera introduces his host and hostess to anyone who comes to speak to him unless:
   a. An introduction would be awkward due to other people blocking the space between them.
   b. The visitor was never formally introduced to the guest.
   c. The host is an opera aficionado and prefers not to mix his music and social duties.

FORMAL DINING

3. The hostess is always the last to go into the dining room except when:
   a. The guest of honor is younger than she.

    b. The President of the United States is present.

    c. She has not used place cards and must indicate all the guests' seating.

4. The ideal staff for a small dinner party (under twelve people) is:

    a. A butler and a cook.

    b. A butler, a cook, and a footman.

    c. A butler, a cook, a footman, and a maid.

5. When a lady is ready to take off her gloves at the table, what does she do with them?

    a. Lays them neatly in her lap and covers them with her napkin.

    b. Leaves them on her arm, turning back the hand of the glove.

    c. Removes them and passes them gracefully to the footman.

6. Which of the following is never used at a formal dinner?

    a. A grapefruit spoon.

    b. A butter knife.

    c. An oyster fork.

CORRESPONDENCE

7. The flap on the envelope of your stationery should never be:

    a. Pointed.

    b. Rounded.

    c. Square.

8. A widow may use the device on the shield of her husband's coat of arms on her letter paper only when:

    a. She prints it properly, as a part of the complete crest.

    b. She transfers it to a diamond-shaped device called a lozenge.

    c. Never; it is the exclusive property of male members of the original family.

SERVANTS

9. A valet always wears:

    a. An ordinary business suit.

    b. A sack suit—black single-breasted jacket and gray-and-black-striped trousers.

    c. A livery consisting of trousers and a tailcoat to match.

10. At all meals, the butler stands:
    a. Just outside the dining-room door to the kitchen.
    b. Behind the chair of the lady of the house.
    c. Behind the chair of the man of the house.

ANSWERS

1. **b.** A gentleman, no matter his age, is always presented to a lady. Exceptions, in addition to *a* and *c* (all members of a royal family), are high church dignitaries.

2. **a.** A physical barrier is the only thing that should prevent you from doing this.

3. **b.** Of course.

4. **c.** Your job is to entertain your guests, not serve them.

5. **a.** If you are worried that they will slip off your satin dress, tuck the edges of your napkin under you.

6. **b.** Butter knives and plates are never used at formal dinners.

7. **b.**

8. **b.** And only in this form. Otherwise, *c* applies.

9. **a.**

10. **b.** The husband is the head of the house, but the wife is the head of his table. She should be able to summon the butler with the slightest turn of her head.

WEEK SEVEN
THE ARGUMENT PLANNER

DEBATE OF THE WEEK: Resolved, that 216 guests can be considered a small wedding.

YOUR PERSONAL CHECKLIST

	DELAYED	SETTLED	MOOT
1 Is it crass to eliminate "maybes" based on income?	☐	☐	☐
2 Why can't her dog be part of the ceremony?	☐	☐	☐
3 Should she cut out two dear bridesmaids—or should he have to make two new friends?	☐	☐	☐
4 Should height/weight ratio determine who is finally chosen for the wedding party?	☐	☐	☐
5 How many guest slots is her mother buying by footing the bill?	☐	☐	☐

SYMBOLIC ACT OF REASSURANCE: Stop charging interest on loans to each other.

4

Counseling: Now They Tell Us It Won't Work

CHOOSING THE RIGHT RELIGION ... FOR A BEAUTIFUL CEREMONY

There are times in our lives when we must consider our "religious health." We ask ourselves questions: "When and why did we enter this particular religion? Is it really serving our spiritual needs? Are there other possibilities that would make us feel more fulfilled?"

This is not one of those times. This is your wedding. You don't want answers to metaphysical questions; you want a beautiful ceremony. Different religions, even dif-

Couples who want to feel truly regal on their wedding day may opt for the Russian Orthodox Church.

ferent denominations, give very different looks to ceremonies, and you'll want to consider the options.

One point you'll want to take into account is how much trouble it is to convert. Some religions, like many Protestant sects, are merely a matter of walking in their door. Others, like Judaism, really would rather not have you unless you were born that way. You'll have to be particularly convincing if you choose one of the "selective" religions.

Judaism, in spite of difficult access, is a popular choice, probably because of the romantic *huppah*, or canopy, that is suspended over the wedding couple during the ceremony. This lovely accent can be made of an elegant fabric or even fresh flowers. Of course, if you don't understand Hebrew, you may feel a little left out.

Many Christian services tend to be a little bland, but they do allow you to personalize—almost as good as being married in your own home! Rewrite vows, have additional readings by friends, singing, allegorical dances, just about anything goes. Try Presbyterianism for a particularly low-profile look, with just a touch of solemnity. For a more hearty "old-time religion," try Southern Baptist—those thumping gospel tunes will keep your guests awake.

Couples who want to feel truly regal on their wedding day may opt for the Russian Orthodox Church. During this ceremony, both bride and groom have an elaborate crown held over their heads—talk about getting the royal treatment!

On the other end of the spectrum of Christian services is the Quaker version. This austere sect is so undemonstrative, you may not be sure you've really married, but it does hold the charming tradition of having the entire congregation sign the wedding license—kinda sweet, huh?

For an especially exotic look, the bride and groom can choose the Hindu tradition. The bride gets to dress entirely in red, her feet and hands painted with henna, and is heavily bedecked in jewelry. The groom wears a romantic (and comfortable) white outfit. The elaborate costuming makes this religion of the Orient perfect for couples with a dramatic flair.

However, if the last thing the bride wants is attention focused on her, there is a choice that disguises less attractive brides. The couple can opt for the mystery and allure of the Moslem wedding tradition. In this ceremony, the bride remains veiled the entire time.

As you can see from these few examples, a couple can arrange virtually any kind of ceremony, as long as they are flexible in their religious leanings. And don't be too nervous about making a choice. Remember, conversion isn't for life.

BLUFFING YOUR WAY THROUGH PERSONALITY TESTS

Premarital counselors will seldom actively discourage your wedding plans, but if you actually make them privy to your every doubt and insecurity, well, it can wreak havoc on your relationship. The issues and possibilities they dredge up can trample all over your delicately balanced peace treaty of love.

The most common starting point for these weekly discussions is a personality test. Don't take these lightly! This is no *Cosmopolitan* Love Quiz. Look how much dissension *The Newlywed Game* causes, and those questions are easy! Scientifically minded therapists and other troublemakers have carefully designed these tests to circumvent your charm, grace, and politeness. They want your dirty linen, and they won't stop until they have it.

A cunningly simple array of questions can tell what sort of person you are. The Eysenk Personality Inventory, the Myers-Briggs Type Indicator, and the Keirsey Temperament Sorter are just a few of these. There are, of course, dozens of lesser-known tests as well. Each is designed to help the couple understand each other, to know what their special strengths are, and to foresee which issues are likely to bring out the ice picks.

Each test begins with the admonition "There are no 'right' or 'wrong' answers to this test." This is a lie. If you go through the test answering honestly, there is every likelihood that you will type as "coldly manipulative, shallow, and too willing to assign blame on others" or "naive, flighty, dominated by guilty feelings." You don't get that result without putting down at least a couple "wrong" answers.

Luckily, such results are easily avoided. How? You know yourself better than anyone. So fight your natural tendencies as you answer the questions. If you tend to be critical, check off that you are more careful about people's feelings than about their rights.

"But I'm confused," you may say. "I've never been an introspective type. I don't know what sort of person I am." Don't worry, there is nothing wrong with being a practical, level-headed sort. Emotions aren't the only thing in the world. If you don't know yourself well, just answer every question randomly. (Be careful not to be too obvious. Don't answer all A's, for example.) When the results are tabulated and the counselor notes that there aren't any definite trends, just say, "Hmm, I guess I'm just a very well rounded person, right?" What can they say? Test results speak louder than words.

DOES YOUR COUNSELOR NEED COUNSELING?

Most premarital counselors are genial, sensitive, and helpful. There's always a chance, however, that your counselor may not be "right" for you. Here are eight warning signs:

1. Suggests the advantages of an "open" marriage.
2. Can only talk about marriage in elaborate allegories and parables. When you interpret them, he blushes and stutters, and can only provide further metaphorical lessons.
3. Quotes extensively from the "Davy and Goliath" cartoons.
4. Places unusual emphasis on the roles of bathing and bodily cleanliness in love and marriage.
5. Makes you hold your hands inside the incinerator so you will know what the eternal hellfire will be like.
6. Holds his own hand over a lit candle to illustrate the strength of true faith.
7. Needs to know the details of your sex life, and encourages you to use more adjectives while you are talking about it.
8. Confides that he has great confidence in your marriage because God told him it would work out.

PRENUPTIAL AGREEMENTS: WHAT THEY CAN AND CAN'T DO FOR YOU

Some may claim that prenuptial agreements are unromantic; but the truth is that these increasingly popular options allow a young couple to get to know each other better. Mr. Frankie Giomotto, a Boston attorney specializing in family law, explains, "Prenuptial agreements allow the bride and groom to clearly state their priorities to one another, to put all the messy management of their relationship on paper. This way they can spend their time enjoying one another, not quibbling. I tell every couple, 'Before you sign that marriage certificate, sign one of these, no matter how fully you intend to use it.' "

These little miracle-workers have no limitations. On money issues, of course, prenuptial agreements can solve nearly every problem, from posthumous distribution of earnings not included in the original estate to laying down the law about who buys milk when. Legal problems, too, can be handled efficiently. Often a standard set of amendments—only fifty or sixty pages long—can cover an amazing amount of who will be liable for jointly incurred debts. For example, if *she* didn't even want to go to the dinner party, who should pay for the speeding ticket?

It's the gray areas that are tricky in prenuptial agreements. To utilize these gems to their fullest, the engaged couple should spend a serious amount of time mulling over possible scenarios. After all, you want this marriage to last, don't you? Here are a few other subjects that can be covered:

In-Laws: Time spent with, money spent on, number of insults (actual and implied) permitted. This should be pretty straightforward, but don't forget to include obnoxious nieces and nephews.

Sports: The bride should gracefully submit to one season per year. Anything less will appear unreasonable, and won't get by his attorney. She should keep in mind that baseball is an especially easy sport interest to tolerate: the groom probably looks pretty cute wearing his baseball cap as he stares at the television, and the players are better-looking than in other sports. Football, on the other hand, although a shorter season, encourages more roughhousing in the television room, and will ruin the bride's New Year's Day

These little miracle-workers have no limitations.

plans—every year. Under certain conditions, the wife should be allowed to limit the number of games viewed per week. Of course, if possible, she should foster his interest in something like archery or field hockey—sports without much television coverage.

Clothes: Here's one for the groom's protection. This clause should make clear exactly how many hours per month the husband must listen (wearing a pleasant expression) to accounts of the wife's shoe-shopping expeditions and lingerie forays. Mr. Giomotto recommends to the groom, "Agree to actually accompany your wife-to-be on one shopping trip a month. This is a powerful incentive for her to cut way back on the number of hours she'll require you to listen. Brides, even in the flush of engagement, are usually savvy enough to put in a clause excluding hardware store trips or even grocery trips, but it's always worth trying."

The position of the toilet seat: Most agreements now cover this issue as a matter of course. An auxiliary clause being used increasingly is whether the toilet paper comes off the top or the bottom of the roll.

Future children's names: The best of these agreements covers the possibility of a family. In order to avoid messy scenes later, the prenuptial agreement should cover any Mopsy, Lochinvar, or Roxanne that one partner may insist on. Working through this particular clause, as you might imagine, has caused the end of more than one otherwise blissful engagement.

These are but a few of the many topics that can be effectively covered in a prenuptial agreement. As Mr. Giomotto sagely notes, "What are a few extra legal fees today for a happier tomorrow?"

WEEK SIX
THE ARGUMENT PLANNER

DEBATE OF THE WEEK: Resolved, that just because arguing is "healthy" doesn't mean you should do it all the time.

YOUR PERSONAL CHECKLIST	DELAYED	SETTLED	MOOT
1 Is "What's there to talk about?" a useful effort at interpersonal communication?	☐	☐	☐
2 Did your counselor really need to know your pet nicknames for each other?	☐	☐	☐
3 Whose family is more neurotic?	☐	☐	☐
4 Does her refusal to change her name have more to do with feminism or the way his name sounds?	☐	☐	☐
5 How is it "obvious" that their woman counselor is biased?	☐	☐	☐

SYMBOLIC ACT OF REASSURANCE: Imagine the perfect summer house to buy someday.

5

Bridal Showers and Bachelor Parties: The Last Hurrahs

BEHIND CLOSED DOORS: THE SCANDALOUS TRUTH ABOUT BACHELOR PARTIES

"I may be living a lie," admits Bob Morton, "but I wouldn't have it any other way."

Five years since his wedding, the twenty-eight-year-old architectural engineer still hasn't told his wife exactly what happened during his bachelor party.

"I guess a relationship built on deceit isn't the healthiest—but I just don't know what would happen if I told her what happened."

Steven Gibson, thirty-two, chose to tell his wife all. Before they could celebrate an anniversary they were irreconcilably separated. Now divorced, Steven pinpoints that fateful "bacchanalian" evening as the beginning of the end.

"Women expect so much. There is this great mythos about exotic strippers and call girls and bizarre sexual juggling acts. Can I help it if my friends and I just wanted to have a few drinks and reminisce? Is something wrong with that?"

Larry Herr, a twenty-nine-year-old forensic archaeologist, echoes Steven's complaint. "My bachelor party was about as debauched as a spelling bee—why does that have to mean I don't love my wife?"

The sexual revolution, feminism, the changing work place, the advent of stereo television—all these have contributed to an increasingly confusing morass of sexual roles and expectations. At first, women demanded sensitivity from men, but discovered they didn't really like wimps after all. They loved the "bad boy," but then wanted "Peter Pan" to grow up. They wanted nurturing fathers who would share child-rearing—but still wanted him to "bring home the bacon." And last but not least, they expected fidelity—but at the same time, when it came down to the bachelor party, demanded that he "be a man."

How widespread are these new attitudes? In her forthcoming survey on contemporary sex-role expectations, Dr. Susan Tompkins has uncovered some startling statistics. More than 70 percent of women said that they felt positive or very positive about their mate "drinking until he vomits." Nearly 50 percent agreed with the statement: "I'd prefer he ogle some babe with huge mangoes than sit around drinking sherry and talking about modern fiction." Clearly, the era of the sensitive, feminist male is over. Dr. Tompkins concludes: "Women have been laboring under the misconception that what they want in a man is 'responsibility,' 'a sense of humor,' 'nice eyes,' but what they really want is a hairy bat out of hell who lives for the moment and enjoys watching cheap tarts playing Red Light, Green Light naked."

It may be too late. Research shows that bachelor parties are ending earlier than ever. Traditional stag party drinks are being replaced by wine spritzers and port. The entertainment is nothing more than a series of genteel "toasts." Finally, men are opting for low-profile party hats—beanies or baseball caps—instead of ram's horns or laurel wreaths.

And what of the Bob Mortons of the world? Should he ever admit that he spent most of his bachelor party playing pool in a quiet neighborhood bar? That no Asian temptress demonstrated the Kama Sutra? That his exploits with the Roller Derby team were a figment of his imagination? Wouldn't it be better, healthier, to tear away the illusion of a naughty past?

Dr. Tompkins doesn't hesitate with her answer: "Only if he wants his wife to lose all respect for him."

UPDATE: HOT NEW IDEAS FOR BRIDAL SHOWERS

Showers may seem a bit silly to the modern bride, but these traditional pre-wedding parties can be updated to be fun *and* practical! Here are a few themes that can turn any shower into a *downpour* of delights!

- "Luxuries for the Bath." Most brides-to-be have a soap dish and towels. But what about those extras that can

Nothing is more important to a young bride than a shiny new toaster.

make a couple feel truly pampered? Some suggested items for guests to give: decorator tissue dispenser, elegant drape pull for shower curtain, decorator soft-soap dispenser, plush toilet-seat cover.

- "Office Supplies." The bride is likely to be a "career girl," so why not help her out with all sorts of indispensable tools for the office, such as a stapler, desk lamp, shoulder rest for the telephone, colorful paper clips? Another choice might be to assemble an "office emergency kit," with needle and thread, extra stockings, Band-Aids, and some touch-up makeup!

- "From Woolworth's Only." This familiar store is a virtual *warehouse* of useful goodies for some lucky girl. Lawn chairs, plastic cowgirl boots, lovely house plants, flatware, parakeets, and pretty good watches are just some of the gifts to be found here.

- "Toasters." There's a reason why this appliance is a classic gift at showers. Nothing is more important to a young bride than a shining new toaster. One, however, is never enough. What if it were to break unexpectedly? Just imagine how a young bride would feel. A "toasters" shower allows the bride to start married life happy and secure, knowing she has eight or ten backup toasters, "just in case."

DRESS FOR EXCESS!
STAG PARTY FASHIONS

What better way to break the ice at the bachelor bash than a coordinated "look" for all the guests! Try one of these:

- You'll feel like Olympians as you prance through the bachelor rites with laurel wreaths across your brows!

- Loyal Order of the Oxen, come to order. Whoever doesn't wear antlers is a party pooper.

So why not dress like bachelors?

- War paint and headdresses! Heap big time. Heap big fun! Pass the fire water, Kemosabe.

- Cheap tux gala. Just right when your bachelor party plans include a celebrity roast. Cheap cigars perfectly complement your ruffled shirts, wide lapels, and *thick* bow ties.

- It's a *bachelor* party, so why not dress like *bachelors?* Dress code: pajama bottoms or boxer shorts, along with ratty slippers and T-shirts. Call out for Chinese and sit around all night watching ESPN and Elvis movies.

- How about the ultimate combo: bachelors, bacchanal, and Bach! What better sartorial choice for painting the town red than elegant eighteenth-century frocks and powdered wigs. Have a little Louis XIV–style *fun!*

BOTTOMS UP!
PERFECT DRINKS FOR THE GROOM'S
LAST STAND

"ZOMBIE": Rum, almond cream, Triple Sec, sweet-and-sour, orange juice. From your wedding day on, a perfect description of you.

"OLDER BUT NO WISER": Dark rum, apricot brandy, golden rum, pineapple juice. Your friends tried to warn you, but you're just too *smart* to listen, aren't you?

"MR. LUCKY": Vodka, white port, Angostura bitters. Yeah, pal, we're all dying of envy.

"WARD EIGHT": Rye whiskey, lemon juice, orange juice, grenadine. Heaven compared to what fate has in store for the groom.

"BIG BOY NOW": Bourbon, cherry brandy, lemon juice. You're on your own; no one can help you.

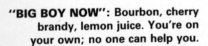

"MIXED EMOTIONS": Grand Marnier, dry vermouth, gin, lemon juice. This is the night for a few laughs, a few tears.

"MELANCHOLY BABY": Gin, dry vermouth, melon liqueur. Cheer up, so what if it's for life?

"ACE OF SPADES": Gin, blackberry liqueur, lime juice. Obviously, here's a gambling man.

"GILDED CAGE": Golden rum, light rum, orange juice, Falernum, lemon juice. Yeah, she made marriage look pretty, but . . .

"INFERNO": Apricot liqueur, brandy, lemon juice. Served flaming. Get used to the taste of this one.

"THE OTHER WOMAN": Kahlua, peppermint schnapps. Indulge yourself. After all, no more of the flesh-and-blood variety.

"DEATH VALLEY VULTURE": Bourbon, orange juice. Sure, she seemed sweet enough when you proposed . . .

THE STAG PARTY LOOT BAG: MAKE IT A BARREL OF LAUGHS!

No bachelor party is complete without a bevy of gifts, and every one a chuckle. It's best, of course, if the laugh is at the groom or his mate's expense. This should be a no-holds-barred celebration of bad taste. Shop early, because many of the rarer treats are only available through catalogs.

Certain items are appropriate for any bachelor:

- Anatomically correct Gumby and Pokey

- Humorously oversize jock strap

- "Makin' Bacon" T-shirt

- "19th Hole" welcome mat

- a "knocker" doorbell

- a framed print of "Dogs Playing Poker"

But the finest gifts are those that make fun of the groom's (or bride's) specific foibles and eccentricities:

- If he is retiring from playing Lothario, how about a poster-size montage of his ex-girlfriends?

- Interfaith marriages are a rich vein of humor. How about an embroidered yarmulke or a teakwood rosary, whichever he is less familiar with?

- Was his wife-to-be a bit of a party girl? How about a sturdy leash and collar? Kinky, too! Have her name engraved on the tag.

- Is she quick-tempered? Every sporting-goods store stocks catcher's masks, chest pads, and gloves. You'll have to look further for it, but a fencer's mask will also make the point.

- Is his bride exceptionally well endowed? A snorkel will need no explanation.

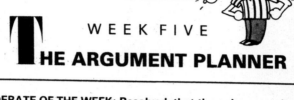

WEEK FIVE
THE ARGUMENT PLANNER

DEBATE OF THE WEEK: Resolved, that the only reason he's not hung over is that he is still drunk.

YOUR PERSONAL CHECKLIST	DELAYED	SETTLED	MOOT
1 Why is having a female stripper at the stag party "different" from having a male stripper at the shower?	☐	☐	☐
2 Is she really supposed to believe that no one made any jokes about her in the bachelor party toasts?	☐	☐	☐
3 Why doesn't she just come out and say she thinks his Aunt Flo will put a damper on the shower?	☐	☐	☐
4 What constitutes "too late" the night before the wedding?	☐	☐	☐
5 Does having a "designated driver" give anyone the right to drink seventeen beers and a tequila sunrise?	☐	☐	☐

SYMBOLIC ACT OF REASSURANCE: He howls like a wolf as she models the lingerie her girlfriends bought her.

6

Wedding Wear: Black Tie? Black Eye?

YOUR WEDDING DRESS: WHAT IT SAYS ABOUT YOU

On your wedding day, the old saying is true: "All eyes are on you." Use this special occasion, when you're really in the spotlight, to let the true you shine! The bride of yesterday had few choices in wedding dresses; today, you have a wide array of options, one of which will suit you to a tee!

Are you *all girl?* If you're the kind of girl who wears three different perfumes at once, so the scent of flowers will absolutely envelope you, who thinks Little League is what

Down to the navel and up to the thigh.

you join before Junior League, then you'll want a wedding dress that's frills, frills, frills. We know pink's your favorite color, but white is romantic. Try long curling ribbons cascading down your dress on all sides. Add big soft bows on your white lace shoes and you'll look just like a wedding present, gift-wrapped for the one you love.

Are you *nature's child*? Remind all that are gathered of your magical green thumb. You'll look positively blooming with a long train made to look like trailing vines! Complete the effect with a specially designed tiny cap of white wicker—the trellis, of course!

Do you want to be the *bombshell bride*? Maybe you've never let the sexy side of you show before, but today's your day to make a statement. If you're a ho-hum brownette, dye your hair platinum blond. And stick with all white for the dress—at least what there is of it! Down to the navel and up to the thigh—you'll certainly make a memorable bride!

Are you an *adventurous tomboy?* Don't let your mother squeeze you into one of those silly girl gowns. You've got spunk, and here's your chance to show it! Try a trim all-white safari outfit, with oversize shoulder pads on the jacket. A pith helmet is a natural solution to crown it all—with white mosquito netting!

Were you *born to rock and roll?* You're hot, and you want everyone to know it. White leather and lace are the preferred fabrics for this wild child, but don't stop there. Have tiny lights in guitar shapes woven into the dress—for an electrifying effect. Finish off with some *ass-kicking* little white boots!

WHEN SWEET NOTHINGS WON'T DO: 6 NO-FAIL COMMENTS FOR THE GROOM TO MAKE ABOUT THE WEDDING DRESS

It's a dangerous world we live in. There are, however, simple precautions you can take to avoid a few of life's hazards. One of the common pits into which many an unwary young man has fallen is a simple remark on his bride's dress.

Once, the setup was ideal for the groom. He knew exactly when he would first see the dress—as his wife-to-be walked toward him down the aisle. He had the entire ceremony, including recessional, to come up with an adequate line to describe his bride's appearance. In these modern times, however, nothing is sure anymore; at any moment during the engagement, the dress could be sprung upon you. Please! Be prepared! If you fail to come up with an acceptably lavish compliment, you will suffer endlessly, tortured by tears and accusations.

Therefore, in the interests of grooms everywhere, we have prepared the following list. Simply memorize the comments, and you'll be safe on this particular point. That way you'll be free to concentrate on other possible disasters. This versatile list can apply to virtually any wedding dress—just as well, since all wedding dresses look alike to men anyway.

1. "Boy, does that dress show off your incredible figure."
2. "Wow, white's really your color, isn't it?"
3. "Is that an original Valentino?" (No, you don't have to know what that is, just say it.)
4. "Honey, I didn't know they let angels fly so low."
5. "It must have cost a fortune—and it was worth every penny."
6. "Christie Brinkley looked like a dog on her wedding day compared with you."

3 BIG NO-NOS

There's always the chance that she'll ask you specifics on the dress. This is trickier, of course. You're on your own here; all we can do is warn you away from three common mistakes. *Never, ever* say:

1. "But I think your belly is cute."
2. "Uh, I don't really know."
3. "Okay, maybe you *should* have gotten the other one."

HEALTHBEAT

THE FABULOUS, AMAZING, EASY, WORKS-EVERY-TIME WEDDING DIET

You've just found the most beautiful wedding dress in the world, yet you're feeling a little low. Why? Because you look awful in it. Well, maybe not *awful* but . . . chubby. Or flabby. Or just a little *sturdy*. Not willowy. Not delicate. Not reedlike. What's a bride to do?

Diet!

Don't worry if you've only got two months until the Big Day, because this is the diet to end all diets. How does it work? Simply follow the "C-Rule"—caffeine and cigarettes! Of course, these may not be the healthiest pair in the long run, but what you're after is short-term results. Isn't it more important to look beautiful on your wedding day than to pay attention to what a few boring doctors say? You've got the rest of your life to be vice-free and virtuous. What's important now is *thin*. Anyway, no one ever said a month or three of smoking and drinking too much coffee could kill you, did they?

We suggest a minimum of two packs of cigarettes a day for the duration of the diet. If you've never smoked before, don't worry. This technique is even more effective for nonsmokers in cutting out appetites, as you may feel nauseous much of the time. For caffeine, an average of twelve cups of coffee (or tea) a day is recommended. If you think you can handle more, by all means, go for it. Caffeine will not only suppress your appetite, it acts as a diuretic as well. Get rid of that ugly water weight!

There you have it—simple, inexpensive, and *effective*. Start your C-Rule Diet today, and be a beautiful bride tomorrow.

WEDDING DAY MAKE-OVER: PUT ON YOUR BEST FACE

To stay picture perfect on your wedding day, take a few tips from artists. For your hair, make sure you've got a rice-proof do. Have your hairdresser apply a thin coat of varnish after he's finished giving you the perfect style and

Make sure you've got a rice-proof do.

set! Make sure the varnish is dry in time for the wedding, though, or you'll end up with rice *sticking* to your hair— icky!

For a high-wattage, nonstop smile, here's a trick from the Miss America pageants: put Vaseline on your teeth. This lets your lips slide easily over your teeth for a hundred perfect smiles! For luscious lips, try Wedding Day Wild Berry or Bridal Blush—or maybe Passion Pink. And don't hesitate to reshape your lips. If your upper lip is a little thin, or you'd like more pout to your lower lip, just pile on the lipstick. Only your groom will know for sure, and he has to be polite about it.

As for your face, just *think* of all the people who will be kissing you. What a nightmare—they'll ruin your base and make your skin tone look uneven. Even powder can't protect in the "face" of this onslaught. Try this professional model's trick: use a fixative, the stuff artists use on charcoal sketches to make sure they won't smear. It'll last all through the honeymoon.

Add a little "wedding day wonder" to your eyes. Naturally, you'll want "stars in your eyes," but who can look bright-eyed after spending hours on makeup? Have no fear. With the miracle of modern optometry, you can put those stars right in—with contact lenses. Choose starbursts or perhaps flowers for the natural bride in a wide variety of colors—match your bridesmaids' dresses, if you like. For eye makeup, you'll want your eyes big and bold for the photographs. Use that eyeliner liberally. For eye shadow, blend several colors, again taking your cue from the colors of the bridal party. And remember, it's your wedding— "cake" it on!

The combination silent alarm/two-way radio.

GET WISE: ACCESSORIZE!

Wedding accessories for the modern couple include much more than ties, veils, and bows. Depending on your unique situation, you might try one or more of the ideas here.

The groom may want several accoutrements to make him feel comfortable and complete on his wedding day. A discreet ear radio for baseball-loving grooms, for example, lets these fans relax and enjoy their wedding—since they'll know they aren't missing a single crucial play! Ear radios, tiny transistors that loop over one ear, can be ordered to match the groom's hair, or in a classic wedding white.

Another accessory the groom may choose is the combination silent alarm/two-way radio. Perfect for reassuring grooms suffering from cold feet, this handy—and handsome—item is designed to look like an ordinary digital wristwatch. But, Dick Tracy style, it can bring help to the groom's side in minutes. Position a getaway car with two pals just outside the church, perhaps parked next to the bridal limousine. Even if the groom doesn't use this option, he'll be happier just knowing it's there.

For the absentminded groom, or a groom with a short attention span, cuff links inscribed with the vows are a natural choice. If he drifts off as the officiant feeds him his lines, he can simply glance down at the clearly engraved block letters (for easy reading) to refresh his memory. The cuff links are available in gold or silver tone, or white with gold accents. Don't let your wedding flop when the groom falters!

Either bride or groom may opt for the exclusive disappearing-ink wedding pen. Armed with this lovely but useful item, the soon-to-be-wed can happily sign the marriage license, confident that if there are any problems, he or she

The exclusive disappearing-ink wedding pen.

is off the hook! How does it work? Unlike many disappearing inks, which are invisible until recalled by another pen or by lemon juice, this ink *seems* to be permanent— and will be, unless a second secret pen is rubbed over it. This beautiful pen comes in gold, with a complimentary white ribbon. A special pen for a special day!

If the bride is of a delicate nature, she'll want to take steps to make sure she doesn't pass out or dissolve into tears during the ceremony. The perfect solution—a small electrical buzzer installed at the base of her bouquet! Whether she chooses "Turned-on Tulips," "Shocking Pinks," or one of the many other bouquets available, the bride can be assured that she won't faint away.

There are dozens of other new and exciting choices available for today's brides and grooms. Remember, a modern wedding requires up-to-the-minute accessories!

LEAVE NOSEGAYS BEHIND!
NEW CHOICES FOR MODERN BRIDESMAIDS

Fresh daisies are delightful, roses are romantic, and lilies are always lovely. But today there are many choices that go beyond traditional flowers, yet are perfectly correct— and charming—for bridesmaids to carry.

Pond lilies are rapidly gaining popularity. The bold lines of this choice set a daring mood for the entire ceremony. The purple flower and rich green leaves are a beautiful accompaniment for a lavender or pastel-green bridesmaid's gown. For a bit of whimsy, how about a tiny plastic frog tucked inside the leaves? Just be sure to warn your attendants beforehand!

An unusual but practical choice of ornament for the bridesmaids is the sturdy apple bonsai tree. The intricate shape of these little trees gives an elegant feel to the procession. As bonsais are fairly dense, they can be a bit heavy to carry, but the trunk makes it easy to keep the weight balanced. These remarkable objects go well with earth-tone bridesmaid's dresses, or, if the leaves are fully out, a pale yellow contrasts nicely.

How about the sweetness and promise of a bird's nest for a spring wedding? With the bridesmaids' hands cupped beneath them, nests are an eloquent testimony to love and togetherness. It's a perfect, subtle touch if you fill the nests with artificial eggs (don't use real ones!) whose hues match the bridesmaids' dresses.

And for you brides that are still kids at heart—teddy bears! These cuddly creatures look perfect cradled in your bridesmaids' arms. Or you might choose Raggedy Anns— their red yarn hair are a perfect match for bright red bridesmaid's dresses.

One final choice is the colorful plastic Frisbee. It's inexpensive, versatile, and it's unlikely that a bridesmaid would accidentally damage it before the ceremony. The Frisbee is usually carried with opposite edges grasped, the convex side facing out. As for matching the Frisbee with a dress, you've got a wide range of choices, as the Frisbee comes in nearly every color. Keep in mind, however, that the Frisbee will set a rather sporty tone for the wedding— don't make the attire too formal.

Whatever you choose, remember that although there are many possible "bouquets," there's only one correct way for bridesmaids to carry them: as low as possible, keeping their arms by their sides and elbows rounded.

WEEK FOUR
THE ARGUMENT PLANNER

DEBATE OF THE WEEK: Resolved, that just because she can name three people who spent more doesn't mean her dress was a bargain.

YOUR PERSONAL CHECKLIST

		DELAYED	SETTLED	MOOT
1	Is he growing muttonchops as a fashion statement or a declaration of independence?	☐	☐	☐
2	How many days should he take off work to help shop for bridesmaid's dresses?	☐	☐	☐
3	Is he "perfectly capable" of choosing his own tux?	☐	☐	☐
4	Is "tradition" just an excuse for his lack of interest in the wedding dress?	☐	☐	☐
5	How was he supposed to know that a golf motif on the ushers' ties was inappropriate?	☐	☐	☐

SYMBOLIC ACT OF REASSURANCE: Re-create—same clothes, same restaurant, same awkward good-night kiss—your first date.

7

The Wedding Cake: If I'd Known You Were Coming . . .

CAN YOU TOP THIS? WEDDING CAKE WONDERS

Wedding cakes have come a long way from the stuffy, fluffy tiered structures of yesteryear. Why don't you jump right in and design a cake that's *really* today and *really* you? It's all up to you, but here are some ideas:

The cake is the centerpiece of the entire reception. People will flock around it all party long. So why not give them

something to watch—a lava lamp! *The Nostalgia Cake* celebrates those fabulous, kooky Sixties. What could be more fascinating than the undulating red wax tempest in a bottle, and by extension, what better design for a wedding cake? (see illustration a)

If you revere the past, what better way to show your respect than by modeling your cake after the *Great Pyramids of Egypt*, or another of the Seven Ancient Wonders of the World. How about the Hanging Gardens of Babylon? The Mausoleum at Halicarnassus? The Colossus of Rhodes? (see illustration b)

Nature lovers may choose to re-create some facet of the great outdoors—perhaps a favorite tree, a giraffe in the wild, or *Mount Saint Helens*, complete with nature's own fireworks to celebrate your wedding! (see illustration c)

For sports fans, what better monument than "the House That Ruth Built," a scale replica of *Yankee Stadium*? Skiers might choose a cake version of Colorado's Pike's Peak; golfers, Augusta's famous seventeenth hole. (see illustration d)

The cake is a perfect place to add a note of patriotism to your wedding—a salute to our nation's heritage, especially if you are beginning a career in politics. Let everyone know where you're headed with a model of our nation's *Capitol*. (see illustration e)

If the two of you are classic car buffs, celebrate that love! How about baking up the *Tail Fin of the '57 Chevy*, the hood ornament of a Silver Shadow, a detailed model of the powerful V-8 engine, or a beautiful replica of the '65 Mustang? (see illustration f)

BREAK WITH TRADITION–AND BAKE WITH FLAIR!

Sure, you can order a typical white wedding cake for your reception—or you can *dare* to be *different*! Today's independent-minded brides and grooms want to make their own statements at their wedding receptions. Follow our suggestions below for a dessert your guests won't forget.

Why not go for laughs?

Wedding Pies: For a down-home feel, present wedding pies to your hearty eaters. Fruit pies are what we suggest, as they are more visually appealing than cream pies. Of course, you can never go wrong with a Key lime pie—perhaps with a small wedding couple perched atop! Whipped cream is the perfect bridal detail on whatever kind of pie you choose. Want to show your sense of humor? Instead of the traditional shared first piece, why not go for laughs—with a pie in each other's face?

Wedding Torten: This is high-fashion wedding fare. The hippest couples will want to have a selection which would certainly include Sacher torte, Black Forest torte, and the delicious almond torte Cockaigne. This selection will look beautiful on the buffet table or dessert cart.

Wedding Pudding: If your guests will include many of the older set, as these events so often do, one option that shows great consideration is to offer wedding pudding, a manageable food. Another advantage of this choice is that you can please children (chocolate-banana is a favorite) and dieters (several low-cal varieties available) as well. To make it suit the occasion, you might have a center offering of rice pudding! Have your heart set on the tiny bride and groom? Don't worry, you can still have them—riding in a small boat in a pudding sea of love!

Wedding Popsicles: What could be more perfect for a hot summer wedding? Cool down your guests with some delicious fruity Popsicles. How to make them special for this special day? Have them molded in the shape of a bride or a groom. What fun!

BLUE RIBBON RECIPES FOR LEFTOVER WEDDING CAKE (FROM THE ANNUAL BAKE-OFF OF THE FUTURE HOME BAKERS OF AMERICA)

It is a quaint custom that on their first anniversary, newlyweds are supposed to eat some of their wedding cake, saved for the occasion. What a wonderful, traditional way to say "knock wood"! Don't be too "hip" to miss out on this ancient rite—and while you're at it, why not make a real taste treat out of the aged confection? With some of the scrumptious treats below you'll be plumb delighted to have your cake—and eat it, too!

The girls at the annual bake-off were all set the same task—turn year-old cake into a dish that's delicious, nutritious, and *today*. When you taste what they came up with, well, just tie on a bib and dive in!

One piece of advice on which all the young culinarettes agree: store that cake carefully! It should be frozen as soon as possible, in a tightly sealed container. Even the most fervent traditionalist won't savor a spoonful of slime mold. But no matter how your cake keeps, there's a way to make it tasty, as the girls proved.

BLACK FRUITCAKE HOT DISH

PAULA: "My black fruitcake had gotten a little tough over the interim, so I thought a day in the Crockpot would do it some good—I didn't know how good until I tasted it!"

- 1 pound Black Fruitcake, sawed into 1-inch squares
- 1 cup milk
- 1 tablespoon liquid smoke
- ½ pound mini-marshmallows (the kind in different colors)
- 1 cup chopped apples, pears, or oranges
- ¼ cup raisins
- 2 tablespoons sugar

Early in the day add the cake, milk, and liquid smoke to the Crockpot. The liquid smoke helps break down the cake and it doesn't taste bad. Late in the afternoon add the rest of the ingredients. Cook another 2 to 3 hours. Serve it as you would a pudding or cobbler. Great for dessert or as a fruit salad.

STRAWBERRY BLENDER CAKE

SUZANNE: "My white cake was dry, dry, dry—so I thought I would liven it up with a little ice cream and fruit."

- 2 cups finely chopped wedding cake
- 2 cups vanilla ice cream
- ½ cup canned peach slices with syrup
- Dash of bitters

Blend all ingredients and refreeze in individual serving sizes. "Kids love to top it with Fluffernutter, but I don't think it needs a thing."

CAKE-BREADED VEAL STEAKS A LA GLENDA

GLENDA: "My first thought was dessert, but I quickly realized that leftover cake was far more versatile than that. This main course is an old family favorite with a new "cakey" twist."

- 1 garlic clove, crushed
- 3 tablespoons butter
- 6 Veal steaks, pounded flat
- 6 slices wedding cake, about 1" × 1" × 6"
- ½ cup wedding cake crumbs
- ½ cup milk
- ¼ teaspoon oregano
- ¼ teaspoon saffron

Fry the garlic in butter, making sure to coat the pan. Set aside. The veal steaks should easily wrap around the cake. If they don't, pound them some more. Wrap them and fix them with either a couple toothpicks or baking twine. Make the batter with the cake crumbs, milk, and spices. Dip each steak in the batter and then fry it in the garlic butter until golden brown. Bake 15 minutes to thoroughly moisten the inside cake, and serve. The sweetness of the cake and icing are a perfect complement to the spicy meat.

WEEK THREE
THE ARGUMENT PLANNER

DEBATE OF THE WEEK: Resolved, that if he thought the little columns between the layers were stupid he should have said something while they were at the bakery.

YOUR PERSONAL CHECKLIST	DELAYED	SETTLED	MOOT
1 Why is a homemade cake "the stupidest idea I've ever heard in my entire life"?	☐	☐	☐
2 How closely should the plastic couple on the cake resemble the two of you?	☐	☐	☐
3 Is looks or taste more important?	☐	☐	☐
4 How was he supposed to know that you don't order writing on wedding cakes?	☐	☐	☐
5 Is there a tasteful way to decorate a cake using plastic cowboys and Indians?	☐	☐	☐

SYMBOLIC ACT OF REASSURANCE: Throw out all your old love letters, without rereading *too* many.

8

Planning the Ceremony: Speak Now . . .

IS A THEME WEDDING FOR YOU?

Most people like to keep it conservative on their wedding day, but if you've always been known as the outrageous ones in the crowd, why not put a little personality into the occasion? It's your party, right? Here are just a few ideas to get you started on planning a big day that's really *you*.

THE BLUE AND THE GRAY

He's from Massachusetts. She's from Georgia. What could better add just the right touch of grandeur than a Civil

Choreograph your wedding into a musical comedy.

War theme? Dress the bride's side in gray, groom's side in blue, while the groom and his ushers sport full military regalia. Have the couple proceed down the aisle—to "The Battle Hymn of the Republic"—through a mansard canopy of crossed swords, with thundering cannonades to accompany the traditional wedding bells. A spectacular tribute to our nation's heritage.

SHOWTIME

With both families in the entertainment business, an ordinary wedding will seem drab. Why not choreograph your wedding into a musical comedy, and set your vows to music? Wear sequins, sequins, sequins! A medley of Broadway love songs makes for a rollicking processional, and the ushers and bridesmaids make a perfect kick-line. You'd be surprised how many priests can tap a little, and what could be better than sending your guests home humming the tunes?

THE MYSTICAL ORIENT

Deep within your upper-middle-class Jewish exteriors beat
the hearts of a samurai warrior and his princess. She's been
binding her feet into pretty shoes for years, and he does a
fair Belushi. You'll both look inscrutable in your kimonos,
and if you want to add a touch of Americana, substitute a
regular cummerbund for his obi. The delicate plinking of
a samisen bespeaks romance, while haiku readings distill
the nectar of love into a few sweet syllables.

PIRATES!

Always dreamed of a life of freebooting on the high seas?
Imagined yourself a swarthy corsair, a man without a
country, a rogue with no law but that of his own hand?
Who hasn't? Well, swashbuckling is as swashbuckling does!
Why not set sail for a lifetime of South Sea adventure as
a buccaneer and his captive bride? He'll sport a tricornered
hat trailing a plume of royal purple and a bright red waist-
coat with gleaming copper buttons. Her dress should show
no more restraint—go with bold colors, plenty of cleav-
age, and let the petticoats show! Either of you could add
an eye patch or wooden leg for an alluring touch of mystery. Better yet, rent a parrot to ride on your shoulder. Yo-
ho-ho!

VOWS THAT SAY WOW!

Time was that there wasn't any question about it. You
took what the church, rabbi, or judge had to offer, or went

on living in sin. Nowadays, however, the engaged couple is confronted with a vast array of alternative ceremonies. There are nonsexist vows, vows that leave out God entirely, vows especially for remarriages, vows that emphasize the ephemeral nature of love, even Mad-Lib vows that allow the guests to play along.

Baffled by the array of choices, too many couples today are going by the standard form and agreeing to cross their fingers during the parts they disagree with. But writing your own vows isn't so hard. Start with the traditional words and then take off with it. Do your own thing! It can really be fun—and it will make the ceremony uniquely your own.

Just a few words of warning. Those who write for a living will take a certain pride in their way with words, but they may not be the best choice as author. And, of course, check well ahead of time to make sure your officiant is willing to go along with your script.

WHY NOT TO LET THE LAWYER IN THE COUPLE WRITE THE VOWS

What the wedding vows may gain in a certain precision of language will likely be offset by a loss in poetry and brevity. And your guests may need Black's Law Dictionary to know what's going on. For example:

OFFICIANT: Will you take this woman, to love and to cherish, whether or not said Merger (*supra*) results in or requires the creation of any lien, security interest, default or any other charge or encumbrance upon or with respect to any of your assets or property, in sickness, affliction, infirmity, disease, and any other debility, or in health, till death, or upon terms mutually covenanted and agreed upon with prior written consent of both parties, do you part. Do you so represent and warrant?

GROOM: I do.

WHY NOT TO LET THE AD COPYWRITER IN THE COUPLE WRITE THE VOWS

While a copywriter can certainly add pizzazz to the staid ecclesiastical vows, do you really want a hard-sell ceremony?

OFFICIANT: Dearly beloved, we are gathered here today to celebrate a marriage. Marriage: more than just a bond, more than just a promise, it's a way of life.

OFFICIANT: Do you [bride's name] promise to love, honor, and obey him in sickness and in health? Well, wait, there's more. For better and for worse? Forsaking all others? *And* for as long as you both shall live? Now will you? This is a bona fide offer. Answer now, and receive this genuine 14-carat gold band, as a symbol of these vows, yours to keep, even if you return your husband.

BRIDE: I will.

Do you really want a hard-sell ceremony?

OFFICIANT: And you [groom's name]? Remember, the ring is unisex and fully guaranteed. This offer is extended for a limited time only and is not available in stores.

GROOM: I will, too.

OFFICIANT: I hereby declare you husband and wife. God has joined them together. Who can put them asunder? No one.

WHY NOT TO LET THE STAND-UP COMIC IN THE COUPLE WRITE THE VOWS

Sure, it'll be a crowd pleaser. But do you really want to go for the yucks on this special day? Besides, there is a time and place for comedy. The wedding night, for example.

OFFICIANT: If anyone present knows any reason why these two should not be joined in the chains, I mean *bonds*, of matrimony, let them speak now or at least keep mum until the reception is over . . .
. . . forsaking all others—got that, [groom's name here]?—*all* others—until death do you part. And maybe even afterward, there's a scary thought. If there's no beer in heaven, I seriously doubt there are any quick flings either. But seriously, kids. Repeat after me. Don't worry, I'll go slow. "My wife . . ."

GROOM: My wife . . .

OFFICIANT: ". . . I think I'll keep her."

GROOM: I think I'll keep her.

OFFICIANT (*To the bride*): And you? By the way, isn't she lovely, ladies and gentlemen? No applause, please. So do you?

BRIDE: I do.

OFFICIANT [*Clapping hands sarcastically*]: Good answer! Gosh . . . I always get a little misty at this point. Excuse me. [*Blows his nose in a comically loud manner.*] Beautiful. I hereby declare you husband and wife. Amen. Last one to the reception line is a melon ball!

10 SOURCES NOT TO USE IN YOUR WEDDING CEREMONY, NO MATTER HOW MUCH THEY MEAN TO YOU

1. Motown lyrics
2. *Love Story*
3. Any Rod McKuen poem
4. Lionel Richie lyrics
5. The post-office creed, moving as it may be
6. Kahlil Gibran's *The Prophet*
7. *The Electric Kool-Aid Acid Test*
8. Cat Stevens lyrics
9. Any Hallmark television commercial
10. A favorite "Dear Abby" column

THE PERFECT WEDDING: SET THE MOOD WITH MUSIC

It's important to realize that music is a powerful element in wedding ceremonies. There are plenty of classics, but don't neglect pop choices, from the Lennon Sisters to the Pointer Sisters to Twisted Sister. Whatever you opt for, make sure you give the organist time to practice!

You might prefer a slow, measured selection for the processional:

- "Here Comes the Bride," the bridal chorus from *Lohengrin*
- "O God Our Help in Ages Past"
- "Stairway to Heaven"
- "April Come She Will"

How about a little romantic tune to break up the ceremony?

- "Piña Colada"
- "When a Man Loves a Woman"
- "It's Not Unusual"
- "Wear Your Love Like Heaven"

And an upbeat tune for a fast exit:

- "Do the Hustle"
- "Orange Blossom Special"
- "The Copacabana"
- "Boogie-Woogie Bugle Boy"

WHO DO?
CHOOSING YOUR OFFICIANT

Chances are you have no choice. You want the church,
you take the priest. You want the temple, you take the
rabbi. You want it this week, you take the judge. However, many locales will leave the choice open. There is a
wide range of possibilities, but whether you are searching
desperately for anyone or planning months ahead, try to
avoid these:

- Any family member. Sure, Uncle Seymour is the senti-
  mental choice, but you'll regret the decision when he
  begins to inject personal reminiscences and comments
  into the text.

- An officiant who knows magic tricks. The wedding altar
  is no place for "Look what's in your ear. A gold ring!"

- A minister of a denomination you've never heard of. All Christians are not alike! The last thing you want in a wedding sermon is a half hour of fervent proselytizing the apocalyptic pantheism of the New Christian Church of Agonistes or some such thing.

- Walter Cronkite. Though soulful and avuncular, TV's best-loved anchorman is not a consecrated minister of any sect. Your marriage will not be legally valid.

If you are still in doubt, choose the oldest minister available. This will at least assure that the ceremony won't suddenly call for the guests to hold hands or hug or play guitar or offer their own blessings or anything.

TAKE FOUR:
MAKE A WEDDING VIDEO THAT ROCKS!

"And there we are outside the church, with Uncle—what's his name, honey? Ned, yeah. Anyway, you can't see this part too clearly but that's the car, I think. This part is some other car. This one's funny—that car just happened to be driving by, had nothing to do with us . . ."

The average wedding video, even one produced by a professional, is little more than an hour of people rolling their eyes, ducking their heads, and otherwise mugging for the camera. A whole generation—raised on primitive super-8 home movies—don't seem to realize that videos will record sound. When the camera is pointed their way, they instinctively communicate by pointing, mouthing words, and making awkward gesticulations.

And don't be stingy with videotape!

This sort of behavior makes it difficult to achieve the deeply moving cinema verité documentary that every couple would like. They'll be lucky to get a few underexposed shots of key moments—emerging from the church, cutting the cake, the first dance, the fistfight between Aunt Marilyn and the caterer.

But it doesn't have to be that way. Anyone can have a video that will truly be a keepsake to be viewed time and again in the years to come. How? Planning! Even documentaries have shooting scripts. Sergei Eisenstein, the father of Soviet cinema, drew sketches of every shot before he ever started filming—the least you can do is write a script. A few more tips for starters: For an aura of professionalism, hire a few actors to play friends of the family. Their seriousness, and ability to ignore the camera, will be infectious. And don't be stingy with videotape! With four or five cameras at work, you'll be well covered, and can go into post-production confident of finding the shots you need.

HIRING A PRO

If you don't have a friend who fancies himself a filmmaker, you will have to turn to professional video services. Don't hire anyone without looking at a sample of his work, and think twice if the only sample he has is of his own kids. Too many "video pros" are just camera buffs who happened to get laid off at the garage a few months back.

Once you've cut out the amateurs, you'll have to choose a style you like. As frustrated Hollywood directors, these pros are often too anxious to inject their personal style into their work. That's fine if they admire David Lean, but not if they want to be the next Sam Peckinpah. Choose a style you like. If it's the momentousness of the occasion that you want to highlight, hire someone who worked at NFL films. Imagine it: the slow-motion shots, the thunderous orchestral music, the gravely voiced narrator telling *your story* as though it were a Norse epic. If you want something hipper, go with an MTV veteran. If sentiment is what you're after, go with a TV-commercial director—those guys can make buying dog food a tearjerker.

DO IT YOURSELF

Hiring an outsider does have its limitations. They don't know you, they may be more interested in getting it done quickly than in getting it done right, and it costs more. Directing your own video can be the answer.

Never shot video before? Have no fear. By mastering just a few simple techniques and effects, you can tape the whole wedding. The important thing is to *get that footage*.

Shoot the ceremony two or three times. Why take a chance of missing the right shot? Once you have the tapes, you can take your time learning video editing. Here are some basic techniques you should master before the wedding.

Soft focus: Make sure to get a soft-focus lens—no wedding video would be complete without it. Perfect for the altar kiss and a teary point-of-view shot from the pews. Also invaluable for slow dissolves into dream sequences.

Inverted color: This common camera feature is too often underused by video amateurs. The sudden change of colors may seem strange, but what better way to filmically express the sudden change from singlehood to wedded bliss! And of course, no dance party shots would be complete without this *psychedelic* feature.

Jump-cutting –stopping the camera, letting action occur, and then starting it again—is a nice way to add a touch of levity to the proceedings. Why have stale old formal arrangements for the post-wedding portraits when you can "blink" the ushers and bridesmaids into place.

Post-production: Of course, most of the video-maker's work is done long after the church janitor has swept up the rice and the honeymoon tans have faded away. Editing is an expensive and time-consuming process, but worth every penny. You'll want to hire an engineer to help with dubbing the sound and assisting you with making optimal use of the "paint box" to get the effects you want.

We could go on, but perhaps the best way to show just how much can be done to put zip in a wedding video is a sample script. Remember, these are just selections; a page of script equals about one minute on tape, so your wedding feature will need about a two-hundred-page script.

KAREN AND TAD, JUNE 11, 1988
A Video

SCROLL: OPENING CREDITS

INT. BRIDE'S HOUSE: *Things are bustling. We see coffee percolating, bacon frying, giggling bridesmaids running upstairs, their hair in curlers.*

CUT TO: *Int. groom's apartment. Groom fast asleep. Alarm goes off. He groggily reaches over and turns it off.*

CUT TO: *Bride's father, already dressed, nervously tapping his foot as he reads the newspaper in the dining room.*

CUT TO: *Upstairs, the bridesmaids are still fiddling with their makeup and attending to the bride, who looks happy but nervous. She bites her lip coyly and glances at her mother. Mom smiles and as she watches her daughter prepare, seems to be thinking back . . .*

SLOW DISSOLVE TO: *Old home-movie footage of Karen dressed as a cowgirl pulling a red wagon, then Karen and Bobby on their father's lap, then Karen after she got into Mommy's makeup.*

DISSOLVE BACK TO:

ELLEN (*a bridesmaid*)
What are you thinking about, Mrs. Forman?

MOTHER OF THE BRIDE
Oh, nothing. Just a little girl I used to know.

Ellen smiles sagely. Karen appears by her mother, having heard their conversation.

KAREN
I'll always be your little girl, Mom.

They hug.

INT. THE CHURCH. *The sound of the minister's voice fades into a low drone as the service progresses. Karen looking into Tad's eyes with glowing happiness.*

CUT TO: *Tad looking into Karen's eyes glowing ecstatically.*

CUT TO: *Karen, her eyes glinting with love.*

CUT TO: *Tad, eyes also aglint.*

The minister's voice comes up again.

MINISTER
... I join your hands together as a symbol of ...

CUT TO: *Close-up of hands, clasping each other. Minister's voice again fades to background.*

CUT TO: *Full shots of bride and groom holding hands, looking into each other's eyes when ...*

F/X: *Background of church and people fade away and the bride and groom find themselves on a Caribbean beach, with the surf splashing at their feet.*

Suddenly they look around and, realizing where they are, hug each other hard. He swings her around, her wedding dress billowing out as he spins. He sets her down and they run along splashing in the surf. She playfully splashes him with her hands and he grabs her and kisses her passionately, and as they kiss ...

F/X: *The beach dissolves away around them and becomes a church again.*

They break from their kiss.

CUT TO: *Organist's hands on the keyboard.*

S/FX: *The triumphant strains of Mendelssohn's Wedding March.*

The couple turns and proceeds down the aisle.

As you can see, a good shooting script is a necessity, but it doesn't mean you can't be inspired on the day of the shoot. Feel free to get those little off-the-cuff remarks and ad-libs that will add a wonderful sense of realism to the video.

Making a wonderful wedding video isn't easy or cheap or glamorous. It's hard work, and it may even make your wedding day a hectic maze of schedules, light checks, and studying lines, but after all is said and done, it's worth it. After all, you only get married once, but you can watch the video every day for the rest of your life.

WEEK TWO
THE ARGUMENT PLANNER

DEBATE OF THE WEEK: Resolved, that "To have and to hold" may be redundant but it sounds good anyway.

YOUR PERSONAL CHECKLIST	DELAYED	SETTLED	MOOT
1 Is a double ceremony with complete strangers worth the financial savings?	☐	☐	☐
2 Does he not want to wear a wedding band for fashion, or philandering?	☐	☐	☐
3 Is a John Donne reading "only for snobby intellectuals"?	☐	☐	☐
4 How was she supposed to know that renovation work was just about to start on the lobby of the hotel where you're having the reception?	☐	☐	☐
5 Should the specifics of the prenuptial agreement be worked into the vows?	☐	☐	☐

SYMBOLIC ACT OF REASSURANCE: Split a half gallon of mint chocolate-chip ice cream for dinner.

9

Wedding Presents: The Good, the Bad, and the Ugly

YOU CAN'T ALWAYS GET WHAT YOU WANT: THE GIFT LISTS

Receiving gifts to celebrate your marriage is a lovely, cherished tradition. Each carefully chosen item will provide years of pleasure, and will serve as a reminder of its generous donor and of your happy, happy wedding day.

Of course, not every gift will be perfect. The lawn mower, for example, that you can't even store, let alone use, in your tiny city apartment. The set of twenty-six official NFL serving trays that even the groom admits are hideous. The T-shirts that say "His" and "His, Too."

In an attempt to avoid these misses, you should register at one or more stores. By registering, you are no more likely to receive what you really want, but you will have an opportunity to impress those status-conscious individuals who go around checking how expensive your china pattern and crystal are.

Armed with this knowledge, you should not hold back in your requests for gifts. You're not going to get any of them, so why not ask for sofas, furs, vacations—anything your heart desires! And when your parents' friends ask for the umpteenth time, "What do you want for a wedding present?" look them straight in the eye and say, "A refrigerator. With an ice-maker." You'll feel better for it.

Like so many nuptial traditions, it's best to begin with a list. Or two or three. Here are a few to get you started.

10 THINGS YOU REALLY WANT
(BUT WON'T GET UNLESS YOU INVITE
GENIES AND FAIRY GODMOTHERS)

A shower with enough hot water
Lighter-colored eyes
An accurate postal scale
A better job
More presentable relatives
Clearer skin
The right to go 20 mph over all speed limits
Your apartment, but in an elevator building
The alchemical secret of turning base metals into gold
A decent haircut

Robo-gift

10 THINGS HE PUT ON BUT SHE CROSSED OFF THEIR LIST

Drill press
Catcher's mitt
Telescope
Radio-controlled airplane kit
Matched his 'n' hers golf club sets
Hedge trimmer
Outboard motor
Lifetime subscription to *Sporting News*
Garage door opener
Graphic equalizer

10 THINGS YOU WILL GET

Civil War Chess Set
A sort of "robo gift"—the label says it will solve all your house-cleaning problems, but you can't figure out how it works

Large ceramic white elephant
"Adorable" print of a cornucopia by local artist
Travel iron
Hunk of Steuben glass
Rococo granite birdbath
8-track tape player
A moose head, a family heirloom from Uncle Charlie
Platter-of-the-Month processed cheese food selections

10 THINGS THAT YOU NEVER
RECEIVE JUST ONE OF

One of each of these ten things would be fine. Instead, you will receive one of these things ten times.
Crockpot
Waffle iron
Fondue pot
Cutlery set
Candlesticks
Cold meat fork
"Cute" dessert plates
Candy dish
Grapefruit spoons
Wok

THANK-YOU NOTES:
A THING OF THE PAST?

Once upon a time, the bride was expected to write a personal note in response to every gift she got. Of course, in those days a woman's life was occupied with little else but the endless formalities of calling cards, white gloves, proper teas, and horse-drawn carriage rides. Luckily, all that is changed. The bride (or groom!) might want to make a quick phone call in response to some particularly extravagant present, but otherwise, a gift is a gift, not a demand for notice.

After all, you already sent them an invitation, they sent you a present, and if you send them a thank-you note, they'll have to write back. Since they haven't got anything to say at that point, they'll probably fill up the letter with questions, and you know what that means! Another letter and another stamp. The lesson is simple: start writing thank-you notes and before you know it you'll have 150 correspondents for life.

MERGE-PRINTING YOUR THANK-YOU NOTES

Your mother, one of those seventeenth-century dowagers, only let your father stop wearing spats last year. And she insists that you write a note of thanks for each and every one of your 250 presents. Wait! Don't cut off your hand —there are other options.

One of the simplest is the form note. Write it so that it could apply to anyone and have the copy shop run it off for you. Not good enough? Well, computer technology allows you to personalize your notes. All of the currently available wedding planner software packages—Bridaltron and MicroWed among others—include thank-you-note subsystems. The simplest version simply allows you to insert the names of the thankees, while the more recent versions will actually mix and match stock phrases of gratitude, general bliss, and reports from the honeymoon trip,

Computer technology allows you to personalize your notes.

creating a unique note for each person. The computer will also address all your envelopes and collate them with the letters. They may seem an expensive luxury at first, but these software programs can save a world of time.

Of course, the best thank-you note is still *no* thank-you note. No one will blame you if one or two weeping Wilmas get upset because their gift is not acknowledged. Anyway, what are they going to do—not get you something the next time you're married?

WEEK ONE

THE ARGUMENT PLANNER

DEBATE OF THE WEEK: Resolved, that a gift should *do* something.

YOUR PERSONAL CHECKLIST

	DELAYED	SETTLED	MOOT
1 How should she have *known* his mother was serious about gold electroplate flatware?	☐	☐	☐
2 What constitutes a "knickknack"?	☐	☐	☐
3 Do scrambled eggs really taste worse when cooked in a Teflon pan?	☐	☐	☐
4 Is putting two fingers down your throat ever an appropriate response to a gift?	☐	☐	☐
5 Is saving all the wrapping paper carrying sentiment too far?	☐	☐	☐

SYMBOLIC ACT OF REASSURANCE: She pretends to let him choose their china pattern.

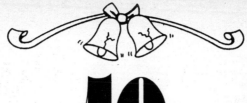

10

At the Church: From Here to Eternity

WEEPING FOR JOY: WHEN SHOULD THE TEARDROPS FALL?

Getting married can be an emotional experience. Don't be surprised if you feel yourself getting a little teary-eyed at certain points during the Big Day. But when is the right time for outright weeping and when is it better to simply let yourself get a little misty? The engaged couple wants to know!

First of all, the bride—even in this modern day and age, with women's lib and all—has much greater leeway in

FOR THE GROOM

APPROPRIATE MOMENT TO CRY

1. When you first glimpse your bride in all her finery, at the far end of the aisle.
2. On the first notes of "Here Comes the Bride."
3. On the line "to have and to hold."
4. As you hug in your first moment alone together after the ceremony.
5. At the reception, when you look down and see the ring on her finger.

INAPPROPRIATE MOMENT TO CRY

1. When you hand over the checks to officiant, organist, and wedding coordinator.
2. When your best man jabs you while putting on your boutonniere.
3. On the line "forsaking all others."
4. As her burly brother clasps your hand firmly after the ceremony.
5. At the reception, when you look down and see $1,500 on her finger.

FOR THE BRIDE

APPROPRIATE MOMENT TO CRY

1. When your father whispers that he loves you as you walk up the aisle.
2. When you hear restless infants crying in the back of the church and think of your new life and family with your groom.
3. When you first see your chosen one, his face an expression of the purest joy and happiness.
4. On the line "to love and to cherish."
5. At the reception, as you share sips from the ceremonial loving cup with your new husband.

INAPPROPRIATE MOMENT TO CRY

1. When your father whispers that it's not too late to get out of this thing as you begin up the aisle.
2. As the adorable ring-bearer and flower girl toddle up the aisle, completely stealing the show.
3. When you see that the groom and groomsmen have all greased their hair back in an attempt to look debonair.
4. On the line "for richer, for poorer."
5. At the reception, when you taste the champagne your mother got such a good deal on.

terms of weeping openly. Sorry, guys, but *never* is the time to break into sobbing near-hysterics. That's Blushing Bride territory. You would be stealing the show if you were to faint, right? Well, the same goes for wailing and blubbering. Still, there is a right time and place to show that you're not made of stone.

All this is not to say that the bride can start the day as a quivering heap of emotions in a flood of tears and stay that way. There is a need for discretion. The his 'n' hers chart on the facing page will be a handy guideline.

PAPER THE HOUSE—AND GUARANTEE YOUR WEDDING RAVE REVIEWS!

Don't let empty pews give your trip down the aisle the blues. Even if you're short in the friends department, that's no reason to do without wedding guests. Take a tip from Broadway and "paper" the house. Nobody but you will ever know how your big day turned out to be SRO.

Nobody but you will know how your big day turned out to be SRO.

How to do it? Discreetly in all cases, but there are many options for gathering a crowd of well-wishers to supplement the paying customers.

1. While you're at the stationery store ordering the invitations, sneak your date and location onto a few other weddings. At least one of the sabotaged sets will go out as is, and scores of befuddled out-of-town guests will sit through the whole ceremony whispering about how much Marge has changed.

2. Invite the local high school to send over a contingent of foreign exchange students to enjoy a lesson in American social customs while they share the happy day with you. They can tell you about the customs of their homelands, while they in turn enjoy an unforgettable and unique experience. For many years to come you will receive letters from young people who still fondly recall the fun and companionship of their "American wedding."

3. Sponsor a wedding seminar through a community college, with your big event as the final lecture. Every engaged couple in the area will be anxious to attend, taking an invaluable lesson in what mistakes to avoid. If you ask politely, they will probably refrain from taking notes during the ceremony.

4. Let your mother invite everyone on her original guest list. This can fill almost any venue, from a church to an arena, but it should be used as a last resort. All in all, you're better off with strangers.

HEALTHBEAT

HOW TO HANDLE MID-AISLE STRESS

You're ready to tie the knot—at least you think so! Make sure your body is ready, too. Planning ahead and preparing a few simple exercises for the church can make the difference between a happy, healthy you, and a neurotic you—between a beautiful, memorable ceremony and an embarrassment to your entire family.

For a relaxed stroll up the aisle, loosen up your muscles first. You don't want to look like wooden dolls. Try thirty jumping jacks while still in your dressing rooms. Gals—you may need your maid of honor to hold up your train while doing these. Then quickly drink a glass of vodka, both to quench your thirst and to give you more confidence. Doctors recommend vodka over other kinds of alcohol because it is less likely to be detected on your breath. Many grooms and brides, however, prefer the more festive champagne, but remember—you'll have to consume a lot more bubbly to equal the effects of just one tall glass of vodka. And of course, a flask of vodka is easier to conceal on your person if you opt for nips later.

If the bride is still feeling a bit tense at the altar, she should try some isometrics. Squeeze your bouquet slowly —three counts to grasp, three to release. Repeat this ten times. Grooms, you'll have to use your own wrists. With your arms dropped before you, grasp one wrist with the other hand and squeeze. Repeat fifteen times. Now, incon-

You may find mental imaging so effective, you'll be able to forget completely where you are.

spicuously change positions, grasping the other wrist. Repeat. Recommend these exercises to your entire wedding party—often the bridesmaids, accustomed to exercise classes, will do theirs in unison!

During the various convocations and prayers, you may find your eyes becoming tired as you stare blankly before yourselves. A few quick eye exercises will perk you right up, and make you appear more attentive—after all, it's *your* wedding! First, cross your eyes a few times, just to loosen them up. Then use the "near/far" exercise. Focus first on the tip of the officiant's nose. Then select something a bit behind him—perhaps flowers, candles, even the far wall—and focus on that. Repeat this sequence at least five times.

"He choked on the words." "We couldn't even hear what they were saying." "She just whispered the vows." How many times have you heard irate guests make these comments after a ceremony? You don't want to disappoint friends and family. To ensure that your vocal cords will be ready to perform, hum to yourself as you listen to the officiant. This doesn't have to be loud, and you might pick a soothing tune like "Moon River" or "Yesterday." In fact, you and your affianced can agree beforehand on a tune to hum together.

And finally, to provide a balance for these physical exercises, try mental imagining. Instead of the tense scene of the crowded room, visualize a cool mountain stream with tall dark trees overhead. Instead of the officiant in front of you reading from a book, imagine the sweet chirping of sparrows in a lovely park. You may find mental imaging so effective, you'll be able to forget completely where you are.

Remember, these health tips are important not just for the Big Day, but for every day thereafter. Make the life you're starting together a healthy one!

WEDDING BUCKS

On the long-awaited day of your wedding you may be so caught up in the emotional whirlwind and timeless ritual that you forget all about financial concerns. Don't! Just because people will be stuffing envelopes of cash into your jacket is no reason to miss out on other opportunities to increase your take.

Sell the good seats—if you're feeling generous you might even let the ushers take a commission on the prime pews, to help defray the cost of their rental tuxes. And station a cousin to charge for parking in the convenient church lot. Let the cheapskates park at the A&P if they don't like it!

Projected Profit: $400–$600.

GROOMS: KEEP 'EM GUESSING! HOW TO MAKE YOUR WEDDING DAY A THRILL

Every element of surprise in your life adds an element of romance. There's something *sexy* about the unknown, the unexpected. To make sure your relationship stays full of excitement and spontaneity, start at the very beginning— at the wedding! Delight your bride with a day she'll *never* forget! Be bold! Try one of these matrimonial marvels:

- Organize the guests in "The Wave" to cheer you on in the recessional march.

- Wear something more personal and meaningful than a rented tux. How about the outfit you were wearing when you met—cutoffs and a Led Zep T-shirt?

- Impress her with your generosity: instead of one little gold ring, fork over lots of jewelry at the altar—you know how to treat a woman right!

- Release hundreds of pigeons in the church—let your love "take wing."

- Sneak a drag off a helium balloon just before you pronounce your vows—your bride will think you're a gas!

- Show her what a "wild man" you really are: swing from balcony to altar on a rope, Tarzan style.

There are lots of ways to show your true love that life with you is *never* going to be dull. She'll love you for it!

Show her what a "wild man" you really are.

7 BACKUP PLANS:
WHAT TO DO WITH 150 FRIENDS AND
RELATIVES IF THE WEDDING FALLS THROUGH
AT THE LAST MINUTE

How embarrassing! The organist is already playing when you realize you don't want to get married after all. Who cares why, the question is: what to do with the guests? You may be too flustered to plan well on the spur of the moment, so it's best to choose a plan before hand and keep it in mind.

1. Try to convince everyone that the wedding was last week; they all read the invitation wrong.
2. Take everyone to a movie.
3. Try to recruit some other couple to take your place.
4. A bingo game. The gifts make swell prizes.
5. Organize a citywide game of Capture the Flag, groom's side versus bride's side.
6. Make the member of the couple who is reneging go up and deliver a forty-five-minute apology and explanation, after arming the guests with rotten fruit, water balloons, and lawn darts.
7. Have an impromptu game of Family Feud, with the officiant taking Richard Dawson's role.

THE BIG DAY

THE ARGUMENT PLANNER

DEBATE OF THE WEEK: Resolved, that a telephone conversation doesn't count as "seeing each other" before the wedding.

YOUR PERSONAL CHECKLIST

	DELAYED	SETTLED	MOOT
1 When he paused in the vows, was he having second thoughts?	☐	☐	☐
2 Why weren't the ushers ushering?	☐	☐	☐
3 If the priest is watching the game in his office before the ceremony, does that mean the groom should?	☐	☐	☐
4 Is it catty to accuse beautiful bridesmaid Cindy of deliberately walking so slowly up the aisle?	☐	☐	☐
5 Was her father smiling or grimacing as he gave her away?	☐	☐	☐

SYMBOLIC ACT OF REASSURANCE: On the ride from church to reception, write your first "family Christmas letter."

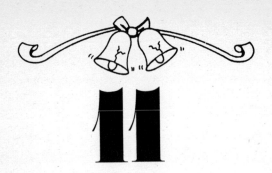

The Reception: Life Among Strangers

WHO'S IN CHARGE HERE? PLANNING YOUR RECEPTION STRATEGY

Omnia Gallia in tres partes divisa est.

Julius Caesar's ancient commentary provides an apt model for examining the usual wedding reception. For even before the receiving line forms, the three great powers will have begun to joust and parry in establishing their territories. Indeed, for these three, the triumphant wedding march was a call to arms. Who will claim victory when the day is done? Her mother, the caterer, or the photographer? The destiny of your reception hangs in the balance!

A couple must size up the strengths and weaknesses of all three, and know what each has to offer. They must devise a strategy and hold to it, fiercely, for to the victor belongs the spoils.

The photographer: The first foray belongs to the camera-clad warrior, for the moment the bride and groom emerge from the church they are rushed back in to stand before him. His initial momentum must be stemmed quickly, or the reception can become a rout, with bulbs flashing endlessly, and poses and held smiles ruling the day.

The caterer: The purveyor of foodstuffs has two powerful elements working for him. First, a staff of waiters who obey him foremost, and second, the hunger of the guests. If he is left to manipulate these advantages without resistance, you will find that he becomes a sort of emcee, announcing each event, moving through dinner and dessert without pause, and cleaning up by 9:30.

Her mother: Fortunately, it is still true, as the ancient chroniclers say, "Whoever controls the bride controls the reception." Her mother also contracted with the photographer and caterer—giving her nominal control over them. They can undermine her efforts, of course, but at the risk of anarchy. When to serve dinner? When to begin dancing? When to toss the bouquet? If she remains calm and relatively sober, even the combined forces of the hired help stand no chance against her.

Stomach-churning rides discourage heavy eaters.

RECEPTION HALLS: THE SKY'S THE LIMIT

Today's wedding reception doesn't have to be in a hotel ballroom or your home. To find the perfect spot to celebrate your wedding, research all the possibilities in your area. Then create an advantage/disadvantage chart. Once you've established your priorities, you'll be able to choose easily from your list. Here's an example of what your chart might look like—with some great new ideas included!

LOCATION	ADVANTAGE	DISADVANTAGE
SHOPPING MALL	Escalator provides perfect bouquet-tossing place.	Guests may be distracted by shoe sales.
IHOP	Something to suit everyone's taste.	Syrup can ruin wedding finery.
AMUSEMENT PARK	Save money on food: serve only cotton candy and popcorn; stomach-churning rides discourage heavy eaters.	Gifts may be black velour posters and pink stuffed animals with paper eyes.
AIRPORT LOUNGE	Convenient for out-of-town guests.	Will probably have to include people who are there already, sleeping on their suitcases.
HIGH SCHOOL CAFETERIA	Easy to find for alums, spacious.	Guests may be instinctively drawn into a food fight.

THAT'S ENTERTAINMENT– RECEPTION-STYLE!

Some couples may stick with a modest string quartet or a three-piece band playing standard wedding reception tunes: "New York, New York," "We've Only Just Begun," and others that all sound exactly alike. However, there are a number of other possibilities that the more adventurous couple may want to consider:

- Stand-up comedy. Just don't let your Uncle Fred do it, no matter how funny he thinks he is.

- A marching band. The advantage here over a regular band is that all the guests get a chance to join in. Have

All the guests get a chance to join in.

the majorettes and baton twirlers lead the guests into the party, then begin circling on their own. Have them form a heart, with the couple's initials in the center. How festive!

- Circus acts. Arranging the reception area as a modest one-ring circus is always a hit. A few Siberian tigers leaping through hoops of fire and just one or two trapeze acts overhead can really liven up the party.

So use your imaginations! Adapt one of these suggestions or create your own for a truly memorable reception.

Healthbeat

CELEBRATE! THE DIET IS OVER!

There's a time for discipline and a time to let it all hang out! A mere 720 cups of coffee and 2,400 cigarettes after starting the C-Rule Diet, you've dropped those twenty pounds. In your wedding dress today, you look frankly fabulous. But now it's over! You've got the ring, he's signed the license, *you never have to diet again.* For your pleasure —and for your health—*eat!*

AN ETHNO-CULINARY GUIDE
FOR WEDDING GUESTS

	Champagne runs out at . . .	Fill up on . . .	Grab 'em quick . . .	Sit-down dinner	One word of advice
PROTESTANT	7:30	Crackers	Caviar and cream cheese	Chicken Divan	Eat a big lunch.
JEWISH	7:45	Challah	Pickled herring	Swedish meatballs, roast beef slabs, etc.	Go easy on the fatty meats.
ITALIAN	Doesn't	Take your time, there's plenty.	Marinated artichoke hearts	Veal piccata, spaghetti marinara, and more	Remember to breathe.
ATHEIST	11:00	Spiced cabbage mound	Shrimp	Tex-Mex	An audible burp is an appropriate way of expressing appreciation to the host.
URBAN HIP	Portuguese vinho verde instead of champagne —10:30	Goat cheese	Stuffed finocchio	Sashimi	Pretend you know.

You've got the ring, he's signed the license; you never have to diet again.

The weight loss you've incurred over the last couple months has meant a drastic adjustment for your body. You'll want to correct this as quickly as possible. Survey the buffet at the reception. Your best bets are nuts, egg dishes, buttery treats. And remember, sugar not only helps you to gain those needed pounds, it provides a "high" to keep you chipper all through the party.

Try to consume a minimum of 10,000 calories at the reception. You should say hello to a few of the guests, of course, but your main responsibility is eating. If you start to feel a bit bloated, have a few more drinks. Scotch and bourbon, keep in mind, have more calories than the lighter liquors—so toss 'em down!

When you hear the sweet sound of your wedding dress seams beginning to pop, you'll know it's your body saying "Thank you"!

GIVING A TOAST?
YOU DO KNOW WHAT TO SAY!

There are any number of wonderful creative ways to stand and publicly wish all the best to the soon-to-be-weds. Of course, if you really get tongue-tied it is all right to simply blurt out some brief exhortation of good luck, but why not seize this moment to say much more? The thoughtful member of the wedding has planned a toast well in advance, a lovingly crafted homily full of affection, humor, and good cheer.

Still stuck for an idea? Just to get you started, here are a few tried-and-tested themes for toasts.

- The difference between living together and being married

- The cost, method, and sacrifice of getting to this out-of-the-way town

- Divorce rates nowadays

- The many differences between the two families

- A funny story about either bride's or groom's ex

- Lessons from the tragedy that was your own marriage

- Modern attitudes about premarital sex

- How unfair that the couple didn't get a *Times* announcement

WEDDING BUCKS

Although the bride and groom may find themselves a little busy at their reception, they should not neglect an admirable opportunity to increase their income. It's not a pretty word, but here it is: blackmail. Yes, simply encourage those stalwart members of certain organizations or of the community to imbibe heavily—not hard to do at wedding receptions! Then be sure that you are armed with a camera. Capture forever Senator Cladell doing his best "pig face," with his nose pushed up and his eyes pulled at the sides. Snap a shot of your boss, Mr. Franklin, sneaking a hand onto a bridesmaid's thigh. Yes, everyone has fun at weddings! A little time invested now can make your future a bit brighter.

Projected Profit: $1,000–$15,000 over a lifetime; plus favors.

THE LOST ART OF SMALL TALK: HOW TO TALK TO GROWN-UPS

You've always been a little shy, a little awkward when talking to strangers. Now you will be confronted with scores of acquaintances and new relatives who are literally lining up to have a few words with you. What to do?

Have no fear. With a little preparation you'll be bantering with priests, with uncles in auto parts merchandising, even having a gay old time chatting it up with some fat old lady whose niece (whose side of the family is this, anyway?) refers to her as "Aunt Sominex."

The reception line is a perfect warm-up to the party at large. Each conversation lasts no longer than ten or twenty seconds, so you hardly need to listen. The groom can handle most of these encounters with a simple "Oh, yes, thank you. Isn't she beautiful? Thank you so much for coming. It's wonderful to see you again." The bride needs even less, so long as she alternately glows and blushes (no mean trick; this should be practiced) sufficiently. To add a note of conspiratorial glee, either one can whisper, "Don't miss out on the Brie and bacon canapés, they're to die for!" These "secrets" make each guest feel special and also accelerate the line.

After the reception line has broken up, you will find yourself in a dizzying conversational whirlwind. The compulsories are over and the freestyle events lie ahead. Stay at ease, shoulders back, tummy in, hips forward, champagne glass held at a roguish tilt: proceed to mingle. Remember, the old rules don't apply. Once, mothers warned "never talk religion or politics," but there is absolutely no reason to exclude these "touchy" subjects from your repertoire. Here are some political comments you might make to break the ice:

- "Y'know, it's democracy that made this country great."

- "Isn't this an election year?"

- "I understand our silver pattern is the same one they have in the White House."

Religion is no more difficult:

- "Churches sure are beautiful buildings, aren't they?"
- "My favorite part of services is the singing."
- "Thank God the heat wave broke before the wedding!"

So now you've made a start. Luckily, wedding guests all want to talk about the same things: how beautiful the bride is, how hot the church was, how good the food is, and how much trouble they had with traffic or their flight. As the party progresses you can hone your stock answers into gems of wit.

Now, we don't mean to say that gabbing with friends and strangers for five hours is without its pitfalls. There is no good answer to "So how does it feel to be married?" Do, however, resist the temptation (after the fifteenth time you are asked) to respond: "I dunno, how does it feel to have spent three hundred bucks on plane tickets for a luke-warm slice of roast beef, some cheap champagne, and a hank of Cheddar cheese?" Sarcasm is a no-no on this day of celebration.

AT THE RECEPTION
THE ARGUMENT PLANNER

DEBATE OF THE HOUR: Resolved, that they should have eloped.

YOUR PERSONAL CHECKLIST	DELAYED	SETTLED	MOOT
1 Should he talk to her during the reception or is it more important to hobnob with the guests?	☐	☐	☐
2 Was it right to yell "No budgies!" when the maid of honor tried to skip to the front of the buffet line?	☐	☐	☐
3 Should he have put out a perfectly good cigar when the first dance began?	☐	☐	☐
4 Why should we leave when the party is just starting to hop?	☐	☐	☐
5 Should her mother have been happy that he supplemented the dwindling food by ordering in ten pizzas?	☐	☐	☐

SYMBOLIC ACT OF REASSURANCE: Sell one of your telephone answering machines.

12

The Honeymoon: A Loaf of Bread, a Jug of Wine, and a Whirlpool Bath Shaped Like a Champagne Glass

PLAN A ONE-IN-A-MILLION HONEYMOON!

In planning a wedding, the bride and the groom must consider lots of other people—family and friends particularly. But in planning a honeymoon, it's strictly the two of you.

That's why you should make sure it's a *one-in-a-million* honeymoon, a honeymoon custom-made for the two of you and your special interests!

Perhaps the two of you are real classical music buffs—met at a concert, in fact. What better way to celebrate your new life together than by planning an itinerary around *a tour of the major European symphony orchestras*! That's right, fly to a new destination each day. Vienna, Hamburg, London—all your favorites! Spend your private time listening to the pieces you'll be hearing *live* shortly, then whisk off to your reserved seats. It'll be a symphony of love—and a *one-in-a-million* honeymoon!

If you both worship the body—and not just each other's—you'll want a honeymoon that keeps the two of you active. Schedule your wedding so that you can go directly to a *triathlon*! A perfect way to "go the distance" for your new relationship! The two of you, running side by side, seemingly forever!

Did you have something more intellectual in mind? Have no fear, there's an ideal wedding trip for you, too. How about reserving a small private *study retreat*? Together, you can choose a topic for the honeymoon, then put your *hearts* in it! The complete works of Henry James make a nice package if your stay is going to be a long one. For shorter honeymoons, try Shakespeare's histories or John Donne's sonnets. Schedule discussions each morning for three or four hours, then read quietly in the evenings. You'll find this makes for rewarding time together!

There are dozens of other ideas, of course. What about baking, biochemistry, primitive cultures in central Africa? Whatever the two of you share, you can turn that interest into a *one-in-a-million* honeymoon!

The complete works of Henry James make a nice package if your stay is going to be a long one.

$\mathcal{W}$EDDING $\mathcal{B}$UCKS

If you're staying at a resort or hotel for your honeymoon, you may have just earned back the money you've spent on it! Check with the manager to see if they're making up new brochures anytime soon. If they are, offer your services as the perfect "loving couple" to be pictured. He may pshaw, but convince him that professional models could never have the glow that true honeymooners do. This arrangement allows the two of you to enjoy all the amenities

of the resort—horseback riding, skiing, tennis, golf, whatever—as well as providing some cold cash.
Projected Profit: $1,500–$4,000.

THE HONEYMOON: KEY TO A LIFETIME OF HAPPINESS

Back when the bride wore pigtails and the only wedding she planned was Ken and Barbie's, a honeymoon seemed like nothing but a joyous romp on the beach. Barbie and Ken went zipping off in their dune buggy for vacation and came back two weeks later without a hint of car trouble as Malibu Barbie and Malibu Ken. It was an idealized, little-girl's view of the world. And it was wrong. Dead wrong.

All your lives have been a preparation for these two weeks, and they can make or break your marriage. If you have a wonderful time, the years of joyful loving will stretch ahead like blissful eternity. Anything less and life may prove a rocky way, full of misdirection and emptiness. Every squabble and mishap, every miscommunication and dull moment of the honeymoon will only be compounded, magnified, and fed by the marriage. A slight hesitation will begin the irreversible erosion of your sacred bond of trust, so newly sealed! A mere bored glance will plant the seeds that grow into tomorrow's mighty forest of solitude. A moment's failure can turn the tide that will forever destroy your lover's confidence. What to do? Don't fret, don't pother, but *do* make that honeymoon perfect!

Both bride and groom know what needs to be done first. Throughout the engagement they have known what lies just beyond the wedding: a two-week trial of their inner fortitude, a grueling, nonstop sexual marathon that will test their nerves, their mettle, their ingenuity, and—most of all—their relationship. Be strong! Be demonstrative! Be loud! You have nothing to fear but fear itself.

The test is far from that simple, though. The newlyweds must also be entirely fascinated and consumed by each other. They must not let their minds stray for a moment! A passing steam calliope is nothing compared to the curves of your true one's ear. A local military coup has all the impact of a soft breeze compared to the delicate way she holds a flower.

Finally, the two of you must forge a bond of communication that exceeds all scientific phenomena, an eerie means of knowing exactly what the other is thinking, which breakfast cereal they want, which seashell is their favorite. Speech becomes a luxury as two becomes one, transported to some ethereal plane where you sip the nectar of pure affection and dine on perfect love. Don't say impossible or you are doomed from the start. On the other hand, scaling these heights of rapture can be made significantly easier by having a heart-shaped bathtub.

HEALTHBEAT

HONEYMOON HYSTERIA

It's your honeymoon, and you should be feeling great. In fact, you are feeling great. You've never felt better. You're in great shape, eating right, exercising a lot. Your body is lean and mean, and your mind is sharp as a pin. You never realized before just how brilliant you are. And your new spouse! He/she is brilliant, too! You can't believe how witty you are! And your eyes! You always thought your eyes were boring old brown, but now you see the truth—suddenly, you realize that you've always had beautiful green eyes!!! And you're rich, too. And you're a painter. That's right, you're a famous painter. You're a world-renowned painter with a show at the Museum of Modern Art right now!

The preceding paragraph is an example of honeymoon hysteria. You can see how quickly this tragic disease takes hold, starting with harmless exaggerations and degenerating into frantic delusions and finally to total insanity.

Honeymoon hysteria and its milder form, honeymoon hallucinations, result from the sudden release of pressure caused by the wedding, after all the strain of trying to be "in love." Although the prognosis is good in most cases, observers should make sure that the patient's case is not severe. The following examples will help, although a doctor should be consulted.

HONEYMOON HALLUCINATIONS AND MILD HONEYMOON HYSTERIA

- All the money wedding gifts you received will be enough to get you out of debt.

- No one noticed how drunk your Aunt Cecilia was at the reception.

- You didn't blink during a single one of your wedding photographs.

- You have a special new rapport with your mother-in-law.

TERMINAL HONEYMOON HYSTERIA

- You can't wait to get home to your new seventeen-room mansion.

- Yes, the mansion with the live-in staff of five.

- Perhaps you'll take the private jet to get there.

- Except you're sure to be harassed by the press as soon as the jet lands—they never let you alone.

- You are an alien from another planet; your marriage has been an experiment in human Z-axis emotive interaction; soon you will return home to your kingdom on Quintron.

- Your new spouse thinks you are perfect.

WHAT EVERY HONEYMOONER SHOULD KNOW ABOUT SITCOM SYNDROME (COULD YOUR HONEYMOON BE A LOVE AMERICAN STYLE RERUN?)

Bob, twenty-five, and Marcia, twenty-four, were enraptured when they arrived for their honeymoon at a Colorado skiing lodge. They were alone at last, surrounded by nothing but packed powder for miles. Both were excellent skiers—in fact, their first kiss had been on a chair lift! It was the perfect romantic getaway. Except that no one had told them about Sitcom Syndrome.

Naturally, Bob tried on some new ski boots that evening, only to get them irretrievably stuck on his feet. Pulling did no good, so Bob tried tying a heavy suitcase to the boot and throwing the suitcase out the window. The only result was the doorman's comment that it was snowing underwear. Marcia's suggestion—to fill the boots with cold water to shrink his feet—only resulted in a hilarious squeaking noise whenever Bob walked. It was then that both of them became convinced they could hear a laugh track. Suffice it to say that Bob and Marcia were suffering from Sitcom Syndrome.

Naturally, Bob and Marcia became anxious and unhappy. For all they knew, they were losing their minds! The honeymoon was spoiled. Only on their return did they discover just how common their situation was. Friends, counselors, clergy, all reassured them. Too late, they now know that it is perfectly natural to feel that your honeymoon is a sitcom.

A recent survey showed that at least 70 percent of recently married couples experienced honeymoons that "strongly" reminded them of specific *Love American Style* episodes, while another 10 percent felt "some similarity" to those shows and 2 percent felt it was more like an episode of *Joanie Loves Chachi*. Another 1 percent cited *Who's the Boss?*

Most honeymoons will, at some point, resemble a sitcom.

Feelings of being in a sitcom are perfectly natural, but what should you do about them? You can't just give in and spend your week of bliss spouting wisecracks and double entendres. Dr. Paul Seed, a Boston videotherapist, advises compromise: "Accept your feelings, but don't let them run away with you. It might be okay to throw in a few goofy double takes and rolled eyes, but if you play to the audience too much, your spouse may feel some resentment."

But perhaps the best advice of all is simply: be prepared. As long as you're expecting Sitcom Syndrome, you won't be surprised when her old boyfriend and his old girlfriend arrive the same day as you for *their* honeymoon, or when your heart-shaped bathtub overflows, filling the room with bubbles and water so high that the pressure prevents you from opening the door.

THE LIFETIME ARGUMENT PLANNER

ANNIVERSARY	GENUINE TRADITIONAL GIFT	HALLMARK TRADITIONAL GIFT	NEO-TRADITIONAL GIFT	ARGUMENT
First	Paper	Clocks	Auto parts	Does his advice to a pal to think long and hard about getting married necessarily imply he has any regrets?
Fifth	Wood	Silverware	Radio/ electronics	Can she quit her job forever if she has a baby?
Tenth	Tin/ aluminum	Diamond jewelry	Air-conditioning	Did he ever claim he was going to be rich?
Fifteenth	Crystal	Watches	Video	When do you get to spend Christmas at *neither* in-laws?

Twentieth	China	Platinum	Car	Just how much do the kids need to know about your own youthful mis-adventures?
Twenty-fifth	Silver	Silver	World cruise	When he says that the health spa is too expensive, is he really saying her body isn't worth it anymore?
Thirtieth	Pearls	Diamonds	Summer home	Why can't the kids pay back their own damn student loans?
Fortieth	Rubies	Rubies	Real estate	Who is spoiling the grandkid most?
Fiftieth	Gold	Gold	Gold	Who would have guessed that loving each other could still be so much fun after all the years gone by?

ALISON FRIESINGER HILL has written for *The New York Times Book Review*, *McCall's*, *Spy*, and *New Woman*. Alison married Thomas Hill on September 20, 1986.

THOMAS HILL coauthored *Salute Your Shorts*, a comic romp through summer camp. He has also written a humorous weekly baseball column and young-adult novels, and has contributed to *Harvard Lampoon* parodies. Tom married Alison Hill on September 20, 1986.

They're still writing thank-you notes.